CONTEMPORARY CAMPUS LIFE

TRANSFORMATION, MANIC MANAGERIALISM AND ACADEMENTIA

KEYAN G TOMASELLI

BEST READ

Published by BestRed, an imprint of HSRC Press
Private Bag X9182, Cape Town, 8000, South Africa
www.bestred.co.za

First published 2021

ISBN (soft cover) 978-1-928246-26-8

Copy-edited by Alison Lockhart
Typeset by Ismaeel Grant
Cover design by Carmen Schaefer

Printed by Capitil Press, Paarden Eiland, South Africa

Distributed in Africa by Blue Weaver
Tel: +27 (021) 701 4477; Fax Local: (021) 701 7302; Fax International: 0927865242139

www.blueweaver.co.za

Distributed in Europe and the United Kingdom by Eurospan Distribution Services (EDS)
Tel: +44 (0) 17 6760 4972; Fax: +44 (0) 17 6760 1640
www.eurospanbookstore.com

Distributed in North America by Lynne Rienner Publishers, Inc.
Tel: +1 303-444-6684; Fax: 303-444-0824; Email: cservice@rienner.com
www.rienner.com

Suggested citation: Keyan G. Tomaselli (2021) *Contemporary Campus Life: Transformation, Manic Managerialism and Academentia*. Cape Town: BestRed

About the author

Keyan G. Tomaselli is Distinguished Professor at the University of Johannesburg and Professor Emeritus and Fellow of the University of KwaZulu-Natal. He is a member of the South African Academy of Science and the recipient of a Simon 'Mabhunu' Sabela Heroes and Legends Award from the KwaZulu-Natal Film Commission. He is also a Fellow of the International Communicology Institute, editor of *Critical Arts* and co-editor of *Journal of African Cinemas*.

Contents

Acknowledgements

My thanks to Raylene Captain-Hashtibeer, David Nothling and Varona Sathiyah for their technical assistance. My appreciation also goes my many correspondents whose comments helped shape this book: Eric Louw (Queensland University), David Coplan and Peter Maher (Wits), Andrew Causey (Columbia College Chicago), Lionel Posthumus (University of Johannesburg), John Collier, Mike Maxwell and Johan Jacobs (University of KwaZulu-Natal), Shirley Brooks (University of the Free State), Allan Whiteside (Wilfred Laurier University, Canada), Bertus van Rooy (Vaal University of Technology), Johan Mouton (Stellenbosch University), Dewey Du (China), David Morris (Kimberley), Paul Cobley (Middlesex University, London), John Williams (University of the Western Cape) and my many other correspondents who wish to remain anonymous. A supporting technical role included Phiwe Nota, Yonela Vukapi, Greg Dardagan, Caitlin Clark and Phebbie Sakarombe. To the recent vice-chancellors under whom I served, my especial thanks to Professor W. Malegapuru Makgoba who countenanced my mad musings while I was at the University of KwaZulu-Natal, and to Professor Tshilidzi Marwala, who has done the same while I have been at the University of Johannesburg. In particular, my thanks to Smita Maharaj who was instrumental in persuading me to write the initial blogs for the University of KwaZulu-Natal newspaper on which this book builds. As editor of the paper, she stood out as one of the few within the administration who understood and promoted the role of critique.

The chapters are constituted and rewritten from columns published in *UKZNdabaOnline*, with others from *UKZNtouch*, *SUBtext*, *Wits Review*, *the Sunday Times* and some other published and original materials. The chapters have been edited, updated and the original ideas elaborated on and offered here in essay form, rather than as columns.

All websites were accessed on 13 April 2020. Comments quoted were received between 2010 and March 2020. Undated quotations are sourced to correspondents who had written to me by email on receipt of various columns for the University of KwaZulu-Natal newspaper as and when they were published.

Foreword

This is a series of somewhat satirical essays on living the institutional life – that is, the life that, to a greater or lesser degree, we all live today, whether in suburbs or townships, whether in universities, businesses, the licensing bureau, the bank queue or (absurdly) when trying to prove you are you, without the necessary FICA documentation at hand.

Keyan Tomaselli's focus is the managerial university. His observations expand to traffic, branding, the World Cup, street renaming, students, teachers and lecturers, bean counting, grumpy old men and, generally, the heightened blood pressure of an audit culture.

Using the griot (the oral storyteller of African community) as his metaphoric mouthpiece, Tomaselli asks, implicitly, why the aspirations of new beginnings – the end of apartheid, the end of the Cold War – so easily permitted our entrapment in new bureaucratic 'structures with no soul'. Institutions, after all are, of aggregates of people, of ourselves.

The style of the sketches, however, belies bleakness. Rather, the weapons of the satirist – irony, exaggeration, ridicule, humour – are deployed as a reminder that the numbing controls of tick-boxing ultimately do not defeat human resilience, imagination or the antidote of laughter, albeit bitter laughter.

You will enjoy these essays, even if you squirm at your own complicity – or not!

Michael Chapman
Professor Emeritus and Fellow
University of KwaZulu-Natal

Acronyms

ANC	African National Congress
ASSAf	Academy of Science of South Africa
BEE	black economic empowerment
CCMS	Centre for Culture, Media and Society
CODESA	Convention for a Democratic South Africa
DHET	Department of Higher Education and Training; previously SAPSE
EFF	Economic Freedom Fighters
HDC	Higher Degrees Committee
IKS	indigenous knowledge systems
KPA	key performance area
KPI	key performance indicator
PM	performance management
PoW	People of Worth
PU	productivity unit
NRF	National Research Foundation
RAM	resource allocation model
SABC	South African Broadcasting Corporation
SAPSE	South African Post-Secondary Education
SRC	Students Representative Council
SSCI	Social Science Citation Index
SOE	state-owned enterprise
UJ	University of Johannesburg
UKZN	University of KwaZulu-Natal, previously Natal University
UZ	University of Zululand
WBHS	Westville Boys High School
Wits	University of the Witwatersrand
WMC	white monopoly capitalism
WoS	Web of Science, now Clarivate Analytics

1 *Hacking through Academentia*

We all want to party before the inevitable and final human extinction occurs. Indeed, the current sixth extinction began 80 000 years ago, largely driven by humans.

The year 2020 was a stark reminder of how close we have come to self-imposed extermination. The trigger was the COVID-19 pandemic, unleashed from Wuhan, China, across the world, from early December 2019 and into 2020. Containment of this coronavirus was effected through a moratorium on touching, hugging, assembling and partying. Clinically named 'social distancing', this injunction, for a while enforced by an ill-disciplined military and so-called police service in South Africa, required isolation between families and individuals quarantined for upwards of four months within their homes, whether on large plots in upmarket suburbs or within less manageable, crowded, poorly served informal settlements.

Though most of this book was written during the ten years that preceded this health scare, the seeds of the ensuing panic were long in the making, embedded in the often incomprehensible and bizarre ways that humans behave, the subject of this book. The Italians initially partied while the Chinese immediately hunkered down and, not surprisingly, the Italians paid a much greater price in both infections and morbidity. As did the Americans, whose president simply blamed the pandemic on Democrats, socialists and China, all the while peddling fake cures and racism. Wearing – or not wearing a mask – became a political statement in the United States. Similarly, many other Western societies partied on and suffered the appalling health and economic consequences.

COVID-19 was sourced to unhygienic, poorly regulated street markets in Wuhan, from where illicit wildlife products are routinely laundered into densely populated urban areas. The spill over of the virus from caged and traumatised wild animals to humans, following similar scary contagions like Ebola, H1N1, Zika, MERS-CoV and SARS, ominously spotlighted the relationship between aspects of culture, disease and economy (Evans 2020). A global recession resulted within months of the virus emerging in Wuhan, after previously unprecedented lockdowns of billions of people. These included global restrictions on travel, social interaction, shopping and, in the settled world, unrestrained consumer runs on toilet paper, face masks, sanitisers and, of course, food, cigarettes and alcohol. Black markets thrived. In contrast, the plight facing the 70 million refugees across Africa and the Middle East and parts of Asia, whose access to healthcare was almost zero, was simply unimaginable and largely unreported.

The financial markets zigzagged, economies crashed, supply chains were interrupted and well over a million people died, with the alarming statistics reported daily, as were indices from the volatile stock exchanges. One often hears about market corrections during stock market bull runs and many were wondering whether COVID-19 was a long-overdue and largely anticipated ecological correction, trying to reset the environment, the overheated markets, religion and the organic relationship between life and death, and the spiritual and the material. Even through the crisis, the fetishised markets continued to assume the status of their own life form out there – the markets punish, the markets 'determine', the markets 'live', the markets have 'sentiment', the markets 'decide', the markets 'listen', and even through the worst episodes of the pandemic, sometimes the markets were even 'optimistic'. Eventually, the markets – like people – will also head for extinction. In the meantime, one might ask whatever happened to the publics who inhabit these symbolic, shambolic and corporeal structures.

The virus reminded us to be cautious about the flippant application of what some call postmodernism – that free-for-all, confetti-like approach to making sense of, and subverting, the epoch and grand narratives of modernity. Postmodernism can only be understood in relation to the pre-post period. Modernity offered a more ontologically stable time when humanities academics engaged in analysis rather than, as some now do, in banal celebration and consumption of anything that goes.

What appears on the Internet is *not* postmodern; it only exhibits the impression of postmodernity. Underpinning the Internet is a massive surveillance system that creates hidden transcripts of every browser's psychographic profile, sold on to advertisers, marketers, political parties and governments. Influencers, advertisers, phishers and weaponisers construct Internet users as consumers/voyeurs/exhibitionists/poseurs/victims while convincing them that they are independent global citizens making seemingly private choices. COVID-19 reminded everyone that none of us is independent; we are all linked in a precarious chain of networks of production and consumption, dependencies, interrelations and electronic footprints. When one link fails, the contagion can become global in an instant and we are electronically disenfranchised to the point of personal immobilisation.

Social media are the new gateways to commercialising everything by offering the illusion of non-commercial interactivity. The ceding of privacy – of intimate details and even body organs and odours – has become a form of insider (personal) individual trading to obtain access to, and presence in, social media. The market – and the way that individuals promote themselves – has invaded every aspect of our lives, our anatomy and our thoughts. The digital media offer the fake promise of personal liberation. Thus does Karl Marx's notion of the global function of capital that infiltrates all human activities remain relevant, even as his historical materialism is increasingly lost from university curricula. The only defence by the digitally connected against intrusion is to limit electronic participation. By doing so, one excludes oneself from the new market-driven digital infrastructure and from the Web, via which the connected do business, entertain and educate themselves. One will lose discounts, special offers and online purchasing convenience, not to mention social networking. The COVID-19 pandemic, in fact, escalated video conferencing to new heights in both business and social networking applications. Huge office blocks and shopping centres of the big cities became eerily silent. Will cities ever be the same again?

Consumption becomes a form of hegemony when we consent to being controlled via invisible electronic coercion. Citizens constituted as consumers will only resist digital hegemony when their perks, online profiles and debt are cut. Such empowerment is utterly narcissistic, existing in and of itself. Individual response has atomised human relationships via mediating technologies that often alienate people from interpersonal physical interaction and from the environment, creating a debilitating nature deficit disorder. Hospital admissions and deaths are way up because pedestrians, drivers and selfie addicts are no longer in touch with ambient, tactile, spatial, sonic, aromatic or even temporal dimensions as they digitally isolate/insulate/instantiate themselves with their headphones and mobile screens as they drive, walk, train and play. Relational digital identities are now shaped by flows of electrons being transmitted between handheld devices. Withdrawal symptoms cause users to become depressed, lost and rudderless, their sense of self dissipated. However, identity and self-esteem are miraculously restored on receipt of the next text, social media entry or email.

Multiple digital identities beyond the corporeal can be constructed and deconstructed at will. Predatory Internet phishers become multiply and deliberately schizophrenic and cultivate targets in the same way as advertisers do. Since psychic lack can be cured by consumption, advertising constitutes the citizen/consumer/victim as needing to fill a psychological void. Gender switching, gender swapping, gender deception, gender constructionism, multiple gender choices (neutered, cross-dressing, transgendered and so on) occur: in online personas men pretend to be women and paedophiles pretend to be children and children pretend to be adults. Parts of the Internet are dark virtual alleys, replete with sexual threats, scams, predatory journals, fake conferences, fake cures and other lures, even before one accesses the more mysterious Dark Web.

A new generation of theorists is addressing the insidious, globalised, electronically led neocolonialism that is now turning inwards to ravage metropolitan populations. All the while, the privileged want to continue with profligate living and partying even as the end of the species comes into distant sight. No animal on earth, prior to human beings, has knowingly, willingly and with such great determination, so consciously set itself the own goal of securing the conditions of its own extinction. Wet markets and overconsumption are contributing factors, long known to science and scientists. Are we really ready for the fundamental ontological and lifestyle reset required?

Critical intellectuals are under threat and the public spheres that once offered agency and social imagination are fast waning. The South African tertiary education sector was one such traumatised sphere facing a myriad challenges in the post-millennium contemporary world – even before the Covid panic put an end, in South Africa, to recurring student protests and campus burnings, though a thousand schools and many liquor stores fell afoul of criminals who vandalised them during the pandemic lockdown in April 2020. Is this looting a form of resistance? If so, what actually is being resisted? And, what is to be put in its place? Or it is just that sheer criminality is embedded in the social imperatives of general lawlessness and wanton consumption?

As a cultural studies scholar, I want to identify four themes that emerged as historically constituting the cultural studies project that examines the relationship between domination and resistance. Among these are: (a) how academics can expose anti-democratic tendencies; (b) how to address anti-humanist bureaucracies; and (c) how cultural studies innovatively offers the 'critical cut' that identifies what needs to be done during a time when knowledge is packaged as information to be rendered transparent to the metaphysics of the market (Chambers 2014: 871). In addition, (d) in light of killer viruses, anti-science and anti-intellectualism, Chapter 10 briefly examines cultures that kill and why this is so. The final chapter on 'gotchcology' revisits the critical cut and how academics can address the loss of the human dimension within the all-encompassing bureaucracies.

THE CRITICAL CUT

Cultural studies, the analysis of power relations, was once a globally collaborative and unique ethically motivated activity that promoted critique and democracy (see Connell and Hilton 2016). The end of the Cold War saw the taming of cultural studies when it became an undergraduate teaching programme sometimes celebrating, but more usually studying, consumptive aspects enabled by neoliberalism. For many younger contemporary scholars, cultural studies became a media or literary syllabus studying advertising representations of power. For them, no new order was imaginable prior to COVID-19 circumstances. *Porn Studies, Celebrity Studies, Consumer Culture* and a whole slew of titles on fashion studies are just some of the new journals that feed the field – often critically, it needs to be acknowledged.[1] However, some students and their less discerning lecturers, ironically, interpret the critiques published in these kinds of journals as technical manuals enabling their successful entry into neoliberal enterprise and the profligate and environment-wrecking arenas of conspicuous consumption.

Other than early cultural studies, no other field has imagined itself as a player in the winning or losing of social struggles. Few disciplines explicitly take sides, though all do, whether admitted or not. Where some journals do retain the critical cut, the classroom has perhaps lost the cutting sharpness. And, while tertiary institutional management tolerates abstract political-economic critique of broader structures and processes, it is often intolerant of detailed questions that address the specific systems and assumptions that regulate the contemporary overbureaucratised neoliberal academy.

Occupations of Wall Street, protests against the greatest exploitative neoliberal roadshow ever, the World Cup, fail, but like the French Yellow Vests, the Hong Kong Umbrella Movement of 2014 and its aftermath during 2019, and Black Lives Matter during 2020, kept dissent bubbling for months and even years on end. Except for Black Lives Matter, Covid lockdowns ended their street presences, though the Yellow Vests reappeared in September 2020. American capital survived the 2008 banking meltdown and, with state connivance, still rewarded the thieving perpetrators for their utter failure and criminal dishonesty; and the failure itself becomes lauded as legitimate success. Processes are turned inside out – all that is solid melts into air – as Marx observed. That contradiction still needs to be examined, especially as it resulted in the 'reset' dialogue that predominated in early 2020. During this period, many capitalists did respond productively and sought societal solutions, rather than as in 2008 to enrich the already mega rich more – though this occurred anyway with regard to the Internet tech sector.

But in South Africa, much of the money donated by capital for COVID-19 purposes was blatantly stolen by state officials in connivance with dodgy companies specifically set up to misappropriate these funds. They supplied the state with life-threatening sub-standard products at massively inflated prices, or simply charged for no services at all. The next chapter on 'e-cow-nomics' discusses this kind of previously protected parasitic public-private gangster partnership economy and how it leeches national wealth in different national contexts.

In South Africa, during the 2000s, many ageing activists who had fought apartheid from the trenches soon became the self-enriched technical intellectuals of the rapacious new elitism. Many, however, are now again popping up as the refreshed organic intellectuals in the post-apartheid interrogation of the new repressive and utterly corrupt hegemonies at state, provincial and municipal levels. This book addresses the aftermath of the period during which liberation actually seemed possible.

THE MEGA UNIVERSITY

By the mid-2000s, many South African universities had become massively mega merged institutions on inadequate budgets, playing catch-up between very complex administrative systems and fundamentally reconfigured structures with different campus, union and academic cultures. Threats to academic freedom took on new forms embedded in new administrative procedures that were international in scale. This book thus examines local universities as a metonym for the global institution; that is to say, one part (the local) stands for the whole (the academy everywhere), though these contradictions always seem to be sharper in South Africa. These new conditions have created the ailment of 'academentia' that describes a state of manic managerialism that turns creative and intellectual labour into stressed factory workers who have lost their once entrenched institutional policymaking rights. Certainly, universities can be run like businesses, but they are not constituted as businesses since they have legislatures (senate, boards) composed of the bureaucracy itself. In government, the legislature is separate from the bureaucracy. In universities, the overlap between bureaucrat and legislator adds complexity that renders management contradictory and extremely complicated (Martin 1973: 123–124), especially when university councils, the highest governing body, mischievously meddle in day-to-day operations.

My somewhat satirical analysis draws on my own experiences of being a student and then being employed for 45 years in four South

African, one Ethiopian and two American universities, and having conducted extensive lived research at scores of universities across the world as an academic traveller. My participation in the operations of statutory bodies like the Academy of Science of South Africa and the National Research Foundation also inform my argument.

Hopefully, my narrative defamiliarises what is taken for granted and identifies what needs to change for the better. Theory is not just impenetrable sentences written in a textbook, learned off by heart and then jargonised by students in exams. Rather, theory manifests in practice. Theory is explanatory and the chapters in this book connect the dots with nitty-gritty everyday illustrations from the academic experience. Consider this lament uttered in 2019 by an exasperated professor located at a private American institution in response to one of my columns:

> We've been working overtime lately making bad decisions and poor strategizing (if I could even call it that), and have let things spin out of control with ad hoc meetings and hastily assembled committees to make years-long decisions. What we have now is a frightening prospect of increasing enrollment, after years and years of declines, but a much-reduced curriculum and a shrinking faculty, not to mention being faced with expanded student-per-course ratios with no rooms that can accommodate them! ... and the chaos that reigns would make a Roman soldier weep.

This kind of institution-induced ad hocism is exhausting academics everywhere. It masks the onslaught of economic 'forces' external to the university that are redefining academic life in unexpected ways. Though portrayed in objectivist terms as natural and inevitable, neoliberalism causes jobs to be shed, it shifts resources and populations, and shocks societies into crisis. Similar forces have been radically transforming the public higher education landscape (Gray 2016).

In neoliberalism, the state's role is to create and preserve an institutional framework appropriate to reductions in government spending, to enable universities and firms to become administratively efficient and to turn academics and workers into income-generating productivity units. Texas A&M University, for example, calculates a profit and loss statement for each faculty member, weighing annual salary against numbers of students taught and research grants obtained. The 265-page document includes balance sheets of who earned profits and of those operating in the red (Joyner 2010). Employees must expect to pay their way. In this kind of academic market, fee-paying students are characterised as 'clients' and as consumers. Such demands are now also being made of South African academics.

This kind of productivity spreadsheet imposes a symbolic violence that reduces everything to that which can be measurable, instead of measuring that which is symbolically and socially valuable. The emphasis on the former to the muting of the latter is another reason why the West was unprepared for COVID-19 (see Goldin and Muggah 2020).

GRIOTS AND THE PUBLIC SPHERE

My storytelling style is best characterised as that of a griot. The word 'griot' comes from the French for a West African poet, praise singer and wandering musician, who is considered a repository of oral tradition. Griots are sometimes called bards and in South Africa, *izimbongi*. Though the griot memorises many traditional songs, s/he must also extemporise on current events, chance incidents and the passing scene (Oliver 1970). Griots may also use their vocal expertise for gossip, satire, editorialising and political comment, cutting critically. The griot is protected by Authority even as s/he criticises it.

Griots function within the public sphere; in other words, the sphere operates when individuals assemble and debate social issues with a view to swaying political action via academic, political and civic sites.

'Strong publics' are spaces of institutionalised deliberation whose discourse encompasses both opinion formation and decision-making (Habermas 1971) such as with university councils and, previously, senates and faculty boards. 'Weak publics', where articles and books appear, are spaces whose deliberative practices consist exclusively in opinion formation, but not in decision-making.

Everyone is implicated in relations of power and exploitation. Even vice-chancellors are embedded within national policies on which they are required to deliver. Those inhabiting micro public spheres – like classrooms and tearooms – might be able to sustain small but systematic spaces for broader intra-institutional dialogue. Some South African institutions, by imposing instrumentalist 'transformation' practices during the 2000s, squandered that public sphere (Chetty and Merrett 2014). The point is to ensure mutual respect, and to effect and protect dialogue to work with and through institutional structures in creating spaces for diversity of opinion. The academy anywhere should be a dialogically managed open-ended organism, open to reset, rather than managed as a homeostatic machine-led factory production line.

David Lodge is best known for his satires of academic life (2011). Whereas Lodge's writing occurs in fictional novel form, mine is written as analytical commentary. My connecting narrative is driven not by characters or plot but by empirical circumstances. Like Bill Bryson's travelogues, and especially *Down Under* (2000), where he travels and muses, examining Australian geography, history, politics and culture, I similarly locate myself as a character within my own story. The chapters critique, engage and aim to entertain, revealing the inner workings of the academy that are familiar to anyone associated with it anywhere, including those who are often mystified and disorientated by them. Theoretical musings underpin my spoof of the ways in which the bureaucracy sometimes conspires to obstruct efficiency, punish employees and frustrate students, even as it masks the underlying neoliberal imperative within the discourse of 'transformation'.

Academics usually avoid these kinds of topics because they are messy, break with convention, transgress preferred explanatory monologues and shine a light on the freaky aspects of the university and the often bizarre ways in which they are managed. Taking them on directly, however, can get the academic into trouble. In developing my story, I early on evaded the wrath of Authority by tactically locating the roots of my analysis within the playful but authorised genre of the African griot, on the one hand, and early Western managerial theory on the other. T.L. Martin's *Malice in Blunderland* (1973) was a prime source that discusses the laws that bedevil management operations. These laws, derived from business, industry and academia, punctuate the chapters that follow – they are my safety mechanism. Martin has also written extensively on post-structuralism, literary theory and satire (see, for example, Martin 2004).

In a different but related vein are the best-selling *Freakonomics: A Rogue Economist Explores the Hidden Side of Everything* (Levitt and Dubner 2006) and its successor, *Super Freakonomics: Global Cooling, Patriotic Prostitutes and Why Suicide Bombers Should Buy Life Insurance* (Levitt and Dubner 2009; see also Harford 2006). These entertaining undercover analyses of everyday issues and subjects are rarely discussed in neoclassical economic theory, which assumes that individuals and markets are rational, logical and predictable. These wacky authors explore society's hidden underbelly, the outlandishness of the things people do and the practices that they enact. Unsurprisingly, the freakonomics genre of analysis has been accused of being 'not-economics' and, worse, the authors are accused of swaggering into other fields.[2] Swaggering from maths, physics and management theory to cultural studies, sociology and literature, and health, is my mad method also (see also Tomaselli and Sakarombe 2015).

The chapters that follow frame current debates regarding (i) the academy; (ii) the educational crisis facing South Africa; and (iii) threats to tertiary education across the world. Periodisations are bordered by specific events and associated discourses – restructuring, transformation, de-Westernisation, decolonisation and fallism.

MY MAD METHOD

The lay public generally associates academic writing with boring, ponderous, unintelligible prose that has little relevance to anyone other than other boring academics. Irreverent academic writing, however, can be fun and informative while also socially activist and useful. Activists change the world. Theologian-activist Desmond Tutu, for example, is fun. His cutting theory is conveyed by humour, such as his take on colonisation: 'When the missionaries came to Africa they had the Bible and we had the land. They said, "Let us pray." We closed our eyes. When we opened them we had the Bible and they had the land.'[3]

Relatedly, Cate Watson's (2016) argument on the need for humour in conveying research results is timely and necessary – as is the tart comment in response to her article from David Jenkins on 'laugh counts' versus 'citation counts', a barb at mindless managerialism that measures academic impact by means of ticking boxes on Excel spreadsheets. If a book has pictures and visual appeal, it is dismissed as 'popular' and if a scientist uses a stand-up comic to convey findings, it is considered un-academic and unbecoming. If other forms of communication are used (like video, art, cartoons and performance), these are belittled as 'entertainment'. Our peers are understandably our most vociferous critics, but when they confuse content with form, education suffers.

Academics are not only in the business of finding something out, but also in effectively communicating information to a variety of constituencies, whether degreed or not. If humour, satire and comedy are the best vehicles for addressing non-academics – or even academics – then why is it not acceptable? Trevor Noah's stand-up comedy is theory on steroids as he mercilessly interrogates and upends taboo topics that academics tend to shirk or to ponderously over-theorise. The form in no way invalidates the content, the methodology, the theory or the outcome (Boykoff 2019).

The illusion of 'academocracy' is best studied using self-deprecating satire, the absurd and irony, as self-reflectively composed by my American correspondent:

> I was the faculty representative to the board of trustees. Well, it's supposed to be a real honor (chosen by the board!) – and in fact I was chuffed to be picked – because one sits at the table with the People of Worth. These are the mythical ones who Make Decisions and Control the Purse! I was never their equal of course, but at least I found myself chatting with the President using his first name! I was invited to their Rich People parties and they treated me very well, encouraging us to sup on their tiny hors d'oeuvres and to drink their fine wines. 'Really, *so gracious* ... thank you *so much* for inviting us,' we'd say ... and for two years I prepared reports about the life of the faculty. It was all a farce, as I came to find out, and I was the only one listening to me ... they were putting up with me in the name of 'transparency' ... I was witness to their actions but was forbidden from telling the others (rules of confidentiality, you know). Now that I've seen the administration's machinations and the board's unquestioning compliance to bad decisions and dubious plans, I feel gutted that I could have been so naive.

In contrast, in South Africa, prior to 1990, managers reported to academics via Senate, in the universities in which I worked. Academics now report to managers and the managers are instructed by the People of Worth (PoW).

Ten years after I coined the term 'academentia', I learned that

Jack Hayes had pre-empted me. On reading one of my columns, he responded:

> I laughed ... I once used that term 'academementia' in a very derogatory college essay about the American Educational System [of which I am a 'by-product': I am a former dropout, but graduated Summa Cum laude and am a Life Member of Mensa]. I am appalled by the 'administrivia', dogmatism, politics and failures of what should be the most productive and enjoyable facet of the World's collective culture. Fret not. I hold no copyright on 'academementia' ... So I didn't have to extrapolate very far from their own title to upset that lot. I actually had drawn an accompanying cartoon showing an 'educational administrative stereotype' with his hinged skull open, and a crane filling it up with 'academementia' from a huge steaming and obviously foul-smelling mound. As you might imagine, my efforts were 'quite well-received' by the administration at which it was aimed. One of my hobbies since very early on, has been to totally desecrate words whenever possible. (email, 15 August 2018)

Digital natives often unintentionally desecrate words. They grow up with mobile media – and unlike us oldies who are analogue natives and/or digital immigrants – they know what buttons to push. Nevertheless, digital natives tend not to know what the consequences of pushing those buttons are. Examples are the University of the Free State Reitz Residence YouTube sensation, since deleted, where a few idiot white students subjected some unwitting black workers to humiliating candid camera roles. Then there was the twittering American woman who tweeted about having taken all her 'shots' when boarding a plane to 'AAAfrica', thereby losing her job.[4] Add to these examples arch-conservative and singer Steve Hofmeyr who sued a puppet, Chester Missing, for defamation. The puppet later retaliated on television.[5] The chapters in this book are cluttered with such ludicrous and freaky examples as illustrations of what the public sphere has become in the Internet age where fantasy merges with reality.

AUTOETHNOGRAPHY AND BLUNDERLAND

The first strand of my mad method is autoethnography. Autoethnography, where the author examines the relationship between self and other, enables me to make sense of the world through my lived personal experiences, thereby better enabling me to explain the significance of what I have learned through the griot genre of storytelling. The self is thus understood in relation to broader processes in which one is enmeshed. Autoethnography assesses the parts that an author plays in social, politico-economic and cultural practices as they unfold (see Holman Jones, Adams and Ellis 2013).

Second, pithy laws are helpful as they provide instant shorthand in making things immediately intelligible. Martin, once dean of technology at Southern Methodist University, discusses 'kludgemanship', the study of glitches. Murphy's laws about why things go wrong hang out here. Hierarchiology sketches how bureaucracy – or blunderland – has permeated every aspect of our lives, controlling, confusing and obstructing everything we do (Martin 1973: 126). 'Bureaucracies are a pain in the proverbial,' an exasperated director of an American academic press told me,

> especially in post-colonial third world countries which inherit the belief in bureaucracy but are unable to construct one that functions coherently. They build adhocracies instead and create bribe opportunities, enable corruption and ruling family dynasties ... Of course no one knows what the rules are and it is impossible to get the same story twice about what the rules are, but everyone insists

on following the rules and will tell you that they can do nothing about it.

This is exactly what has occurred in South Africa. As will become clear, few take responsibility for their actions and everything is negotiable. The ad hocracy in South Africa is akin to tendrepreneurship, or 'Zuptanomics', discussed in the pages that follow. The Peter Principle, which explains why managers rise up to their level of incompetence, is located in this category. In addition, Martin's Law of Committees (Martin 1973: 79) states that a committee is a group of people who, individually, can do nothing, but collectively can meet and decide that nothing can be done. Faculty and school boards especially are now predominantly based on this assumption, as what is to be done is already decided by the PoW.

'Fuglemanship' is the art and science of leadership or of (mis) management. The mischievous Machiavelli is this category's pre-eminent character. This founder of modern political science was cunning and duplicitous, traits that identify politicians, deans and vice-chancellors everywhere. Lastly, academocracy is the study of educational bureaucracy. Though Martin's book was written at an earlier, slower, analogue time when the academy used typewriters, paper and filing cabinets, the principles remain the same.

Hacking through academementia is the objective of my book. Whereas *academocracy* means academic democracy (see Martin 1973: 113), *academementia* signifies collective psychosis. Academementia describes the institution globally as the sane are not always running the academic asylum – if they ever did. When vice-chancellors, deputy vice-chancellors and managers are not accomplishing useful work, the individual social actor exhibits 'the Final Placement Syndrome' (cited in Martin 1973: 59). My conclusion is that we have now reached this Placement when enough is enough.[6]

Notes

1. The porn industry subverted the journal by setting up 'Fuck Studies' sites, which depict sexual acts supposedly performed by co-eds, teenagers and tutors in educational settings. For every serious analysis done by academics, there is an opportunistic reaction by those who come under their critical gaze

2. Read more at: https://en.wikipedia.org/wiki/Freakonomics

3. Read more at: https://www.brainyquote.com/quotes/quotes/d/desmondtut107531.html

4. Read more at: http://www.thejournal.ie/single-tweet-lost-people-jobs-2095650-May2015/

5. See news report at: https://www.youtube.com/watch?v=dWbO1ngeLmo

6. Read more at: https://jour14.wordpress.com/2014/12/07/the-final-placement-syndrome-or-when-enough-is-enough/

2 Cash Cows, E-cow-nomics and Branding

South African universities after 1990 introduced 'cash cow' discourse to committee discussions in the search for internal fiscal coherence and in securing external income streams to complement declining state subsidies. Two decades later, a very vocal and exceptionally well-organised group of students imported, via the Economic Freedom Fighters (EFF) military-style command structure, an instrumentalist reading of Frantz Fanon as the legitimating philosophy to justify their privileged new class positions. They presented themselves as the disadvantaged vanguard fighting an imagined struggle against continuing colonialism even as they aided and abetted new forms of it.

Whereas freakonomics questions conventional wisdom, explaining anomalies, 'e-cow-nomics' describes different and reductive economic models with cow metaphors, here adapted from a poster published on the Web.[1] In expanding it considerably, I have added my own examples. I am, of course, mindful of Fanon's (1963) general warnings about postcolonial regimes where nationalisation is the mechanism used to transfer to the new postcolonial elite the unfair advantages inherited from the previous colonial period.

In such instances, the 'new class', as Karl Marx labelled it, which arose from the ranks of the previously oppressed, subverts the state, looting it for its own private benefit, progressing from ultra-nationalism to chauvinism and, finally, to racism. As Imraan Buccus (2019) concludes, reading Fanon today 'immediately takes one's mind to the disaster unfolding at Eskom, SAA [South African Airways], the SABC [South African Broadcasting Corporation] and Transnet'. To this list, one might add the South African Revenue Services, the

South African Police Service and hundreds of other state-owned enterprises (SOEs) that comprised 39 per cent of the South African national economy during the decade dominated by Jacob Zuma and an economics colloquially known as as 'Zuptanomics'. This was a period when capture of the state and SOEs by criminal elements claiming African National Congress (ANC) allegiance during Zuma's presidency was at its height. Buccus further observes that Fanon's 'account of an elite shamelessly stealing from the poor, while the poor turn on each other, reads as if it were written yesterday. The Zuma faction of the ANC, the EFF and Black Land First are precisely the people Fanon warned us against.' Earlier, Helen Zille had made related points:

> Over the past few years, a tectonic shift has occurred in South African politics. The Mandela era has come to an end. Emerging, from the epicentre of universities, is a new set of ideas rooted in Frantz Fanon's writings and codified in 'critical race theory' that regards 'whiteness' and 'whites' as the key obstacles to the progress of black people in South Africa. (Zille 2017)

It is from this discourse that myths like 'white monopoly capitalism' (WMC) were cynically manufactured by the Zuma and EFF factions of the new elite's British-based public relations company. Bell Pottinger had substituted the institutional administrative practice of 'transformation' with the emotive un-implementable populist rhetoric of 'decolonisation'. No matter, within some universities, now, our so-called performance management contracts even ask academics to list their 'decolonisation' activities. This deflates what has become a sustained populist attack on academic institutions by those who reductively read only one dimension of Fanon's work.

This is not the place to engage with the very complex debates about 'whiteness' and critical race theory. My discussion does, however, go the core of the mobilising reductionisms that underpin much current populist theorisation.

To return to the poster, 'Economics Models Explained' with cows. In socialism, you have two cows. You donate one to your neighbour. But your neighbour feels entitled to your other cow. See also Zuptanomics, where the taxpayer has been milked to pay for corruption.

In communism, the state takes both cows, provides some milk and you queue for everything else.

In fascism, the state takes both cows and sells you some milk.

In Nazism, the state takes both cows and shoots you.

Bureaucratism is where the state expropriates both cows, shoots one, milks the other and then throws the milk away.

In apartheid-agri-nomics, the state created a milk board. The board sold the milk overseas at an inflated price. The government warehoused the remaining milk to homogenise local prices. No one bought the milk because it was too expensive – this is known as export parity pricing. When the warehouse reached storage capacity, the milk was dumped at less than cost price on the local market, which was then glutted. Everyone pigged out on the sudden – if temporary – supply. Purchases of freezers went through roof as the white consumers with electricity hoarded the cheap stuff, knowing that the price would soon escalate when the state's warehouses became empty. Similarly, Eskom, the national electricity supply company, reserved for itself the sole right to distribute electricity, and other providers were required to supply Eskom only, which has resulted in regular power outages known as loadshedding. The South African research economy operates like a little like this through a procedure known as accreditation-nomics (see Chapter 6).

Traditional capitalism: you sell one cow and buy a bull. The herd multiplies and the economy grows. You sell them and retire on the income. You can also sell a bull to Cyril Ramaphosa for R18 million.

American corporation and university neoliberalism: you sell one cow and force the other to produce the milk of four cows. Later, you employ an expensive consultant to find out why the second cow has died. Universities' human resources divisions now try to keep the overwhelmed academic cows producing by imposing 'wellness' and 'talent management' campaigns on exhausted staff/cows. They have developed their own lingo to keep us all compliant (see Chapter 3, especially fuglemanship.)

Australian corporation: making a small fortune is easy. You just start with a large one. A hundred cows become two. Just ask Woolworths and Pick n Pay who lost their shirts in the land of Oz (as Australians call it).

British capitalism after Brexit is now known as confused cowszit and no one knows how the cows can be brought back to the United Kingdom, where they will inevitably contract mad cow disease and Scotland might regain its independence. A pitched military battle led by a Braveheart descendant will not be required.

Chinese corporation: you have 300 people milking two cows. You claim that you have full employment and high bovine productivity. The journalists who report the real situation are sent to re-education camps.

In South Africa, we have the perpetually insolvent SOEs, each bloated with fraudsters, unproductive staff and endless price increases tailored to failing service and ruinous strikes. Perpetual government bail-outs milk the taxpayers dry. The journalists and whistleblowers who exposed this state of affairs were not re-educated, but neither were their exposés used in court.

Enron venture capitalism: you sell three cows to your publicly listed company using letters of credit opened by your deployed cadre-in-arms at the bank. You then execute a debt/equity swap with an associated general offer so that you get four cows back, with a tax exemption for five cows.

In the South African Zuptanomics case, you sell one cow to buy an Eskom CEO, leaving you with nine cows. The cows will graze at the

Guptas' Saxonwold shebeen where they will be milked to the hilt.[2] The gullible public buys your bull (but not the opposition or one-time Zupta-fired finance minister Pravin Gordhan). This was the VBS Mutual Bank, EFF-linked model also that bankrupted municipalities across the country, and which bailed out Nkandla, Zuma's huge illegally state-funded, private, rural Zululand residence, once occupied by a single goat and a 'fire pool'.

French corporation, opposition to: you go on strike wearing yellow vests and block the roads for years on end because you want three cows, a 30-hour working week and early retirement. COVID-19 temporarily forced the Yellow Vests back indoors.

Japanese corporation: you redesign the two cows so that they are miniaturised and produce twenty times the volume of milk. You then create a clever cow cartoon called 'Cowkimmon' and market it worldwide.

German corporation: you engineer the two cows so they live for 100 years, eat once a month and milk themselves. VW tried this with cheating on diesel emissions, failed, were fined by the American government and had to put 480 000 polluting cars out to pasture. This economy is known also as 'dieselgate'.

Indian corporation: You worship the cows and let them have right of way, unlike in southern Africa where cows just get in the way. Here, the Indian-originated Guptas re-established indentured labour (Sundaram 2018) 100 years after the demise of British colonialism and milked the state totally dry within the framework of Zuptanomics before hurriedly decamping to the Middle East.

Iraqi corporation under Saddam Hussein: America and the United Kingdom complain that you have lots of cows. You tell them that you have none. They don't believe you so they bomb you to smithereens. You still have no cows but at least you are now a democracy.

Translated to South African universities, where anti-apartheid campuses once actually did apply democracy, some new managers refused to believe it so, like the new local 'struggle' owner of Independent Newspapers, they 'transformed' universities into autocracies and adhocracies, while simultaneously claiming to be liberating them from residual regressive and repressive racist elements (see Chapter 3).

Italian corporation: you do not know where the two cows are. You have an expresso (without milk). COVID-19 closes the coffee shops, so you sing to each other from your respective residences across the empty streets.

Lesotho capitalism: the cows were raided from South Africa. They will produce milk to sell to South Africans.

Nigerian capitalism: the cows are fake, sold online via a 419-cow swindle. You will never get your money back or see the cows. You will just be milked (see also the section on predatory publications, Chapter 6).

South African international corporation: The cows are chimeras entered onto fictional balance sheets audited by incompetent international firms like KPMG and Deloitte and Touche and are carved up to pay for massive debts incurred globally. Just ask the Steinhoff business rescue firm (see Styan 2018). There is no milk to be had. Then, learning nothing, universities employed these suspect auditing firms that had aided state capture enabled by Zuptanomics to audit their own institutions and their staff's financial interests. Who was capturing whom?

Subsections of South African capitalism / elitism / corruption include:

- Black economic empowerment (BEE): both cows were stolen by colonialists from 'the people'. They must be returned. The repossessed cows will be sacrificed in thanks to the ancestors. Then there will be no cows but equity will be established and redistribution that ensures the poverty of the majority will be ensured. In other words, no milk is produced. Think of the annual burning seasons at universities, schools and civic amenities. Nothing good can come from this kind of vandalism (see: whole book).

- Zuptanomics: The two cows multiplied via state capture and the 103 000 taxpayers earning R1.5 million or more after 2018 were milked by the Guptas / Zuptas in Gordhanomics to pay for continued corruption, rather than corruption being eliminated to buy more cows. This is known as the C-curve, or cow appreciation from shoe salesmen to absconded billionaires (the Guptas) now living in Doha.

- Zuma's capitalism: Fire the minister of finance, write off R171 billion from the Johannesburg Stock Exchange at the end of 2016 and then claim that the cows were stolen by WMC, the figment of the Bell Pottinger public relations crusade that had tapped into the 'vitriolic race invective' that was coursing through South Africa's body politic at the time (Zille 2017). The Democratic Alliance later brought a court action in London that put this errant WMC firm into receivership.

- Molefenomics (after Brian Molefe): the state-capture condition brought about by Guptanomics, which positions former SOE CEOs as Gupta-cow-lap-to-nomics. Replace him with a white turnaround corporate expert who rescues Eskom, delivers electricity and reduces corruption, but mis-citing Fanon, scream (or moo) racism and complain about the alleged extension of WMC. Relevant to this section is Peter's Law of Compulsive Incompetence: this occurs when the fired CEOs of failed SOEs 'sidestep into another hierarchy and reach, in that environment, that level of incompetence that they could not find in the old' (Laurence and Hull 1969: 101). This applies to Cabinet reshuffles also. However, the best South African university vice-chancellors, utterly exhausted by state incompetence

and tired of being fire fighters under endless siege, take
up peaceful overseas posts, while the less employable
vice-chancellors and deputy vice-chancellors engage in the
domestic side-step shuffle.

- JuJu's EFF (Julius Malema) capitalism: A financial genius
  who knows all about the wonders of cow trust funds, the
  VBS Mutual Bank and successful tax avoidance and whose
  reading of Fanon is one-dimensional. His cows never come
  home because they might be seized by the Asset Forfeiture
  Unit.

Soviet corporation: you count the cows and learn that you have five.
You count them again and learn that you have 42. You count them
again and learn that you have two cows. You stop counting cows and
have another bottle of vodka. Eventually, the economy collapses (see
Chapter 4).

Swiss corporation: you have 5 000 cows. None of them belongs to
you. You charge the owners for storing them. You put the proceeds in
a numbered account.

Swaziland (Eswatini) state capitalism: all cows belong to the king.
But he also wants your daughter as his 24th wife.

Trump-o-nomics: the same as Australian corporation but littered
with insults against Moslems, Mexicans, media, women, Democrats,
Mitt Romney, China-centrism and foreign viruses. His malignant
narcissistic cows will come home when the Republican Party realise
that it has been cow-duped. 'Bad.'

Fox TV Corporation: More rabid than Trump, if that is possible.
They report as truth fake news like the Bowling Green Cow Massacre
and Putin-the-cow-killer. Moreover, the station's more rabid anchors
set both domestic and foreign policy, which is then parroted/
tweeted by Trump. They also initially blamed the COVID-19 virus
on Democrats and the Chinese, then touted fake cures, forgetting that
HIV first manifested in the United States. Russian TV is an ally of

Fox. They drink beer together at the Fox & Sickle when lockdowns are lifted.

Zimbabwean capitalism: there are no cows because they have all been sold to buy foreign currency. Zim dollars are used as wallpaper.

The sections that follow apply some of these quirky definitions in the world of academentia.

COWS, UNIVERSITIES AND BRANDING

There is no direct relationship between the quality of an educational programme and its cost (Terman's Law, cited in Martin 1973: 57) and 'an awful lot of money is wasted on every college campus' (Bowker, cited in Martin 1973: 57). Agreeing, the University of the Western Cape's professor of government, John Williams, confirms that 'universities have funds to beautify, badging every door, yet under-invest in graduate students'. Williams suggests that the Department of Higher Education and Training (DHET) should rank campuses in terms of beauty 'as this is the latest fad of "branding" – remember, slaves and animals used to be branded by farmers'.

Branding is not just a badge. It is a shorthand sign that communicates institutional personality, its values and the reliability of its product (the milk) – research, knowledge and graduates. The New Name Universities erased institutional histories prior to 2004 and suppressed mention of their apartheid-era vice-chancellors, even if they were anti-apartheid activists. This was the new monologue. For me, it is better to be historically aware to deal with the new anti-histories that displace the first generation of self-styled liberators, some of whom triumphantly and with great fanfare occupied their extravagantly refurbished vice-chancellors and deputy vice-chancellors offices. This period also witnessed the battle of the brands as different universities now competed with each other for profile, professors and graduate students in an open market. And, corporatisation – trading as 'transformation' – ran riot.

The next section shows how many of the new cow herders, the vice-chancellors or People of Worth (PoW), dealt with the cows that were alleged to have resisted transformation.

THE NEW MATHS AND TRANSFORMATION

Political economy analyses usually focus on ownership and control; acquisitions, mergers and monopoly; divestment and fracturing; cross-ownership, transnational acquisitions; state proprietorship, liberalisation and privatisation; supply and value chains; and internationalisation and regionalisation. An important dimension is that of power and the political structures that wield it. Structures are dualities that include constraining rules and enabling resources: 'Structure both constitutes action and is reproduced by it. ... Structuration therefore describes a process by which structures are constituted out of human agency, even as they provide the very medium of that constitution' (Mosco 1996: 212). As the most influential of all nineteenth-century political economists, Karl Marx, reminds, people make history, but not under conditions of their own making.

All economic sectors were restructured and transformed in a number of different ways, enabled by the South African Constitution as a unified nation in for the first time in 1994. In immediate 'post-apartheid' parlance, 'transformation', when people do make 'history', implies the adaption and reformation of institutions, in public and private sectors, to accommodate changes in political culture. The years 1994 to 2000 witnessed rapid and often contradictory attempts to alter structures of ownership and control, of employment and budgetary allocation, of managerial style and corporate culture. The prevailing ethos during Nelson Mandela's presidency indeed was a 'democratizing transformation' (Teer-Tomaselli 2011: 134). After 1994, universities, public corporations and government departments reviewed their mandates, composed mission and vision charters and re-oriented the compositions of their workforces and client bases. All of the crude e-cow-nomics definitions and associated practices were operative at the time as jostling ideological constituencies and class fractions battled out the future structure and ownership and control of the country's political economy.

The practice of 'transformation' during the 1990s had substance. However, the outcome just ten years later was a narrow sectionalism; a crude re-racialisation accompanied by sloganeering and discourses of entitlement in place of analysis and restructuration. Transformative managerialism enabled neoliberal solutions to be beguilingly enacted. The new society that emerged created the conditions for a new self-serving gangster ruling class applying Zuptanomics (2009–2017) of often incompetent, corrupt, lazy, overpaid and over-resourced politicians and bureaucrats who became the cunning comprador bourgeoisies to the new rapacious and corrupt elite, enriching international criminal syndicates masquerading as legitimate firms (Pauw 2017; Swilling 2017; see also Fanon 1963).

In brief, at home, the term, 'transformation' was hijacked to engineer a proportional labour market crudely predicated on racial demand and supply. As Alexander Johnston (2014: 297) puts it, the Employment Equity Act of 2011 imposed racial headcounts as the primary criterion for meeting employment redistribution as one leg of 'transformation'. These were to now mechanistically reflect national demographic racial distributions rather than provincial ones. If 'coloureds' are oversupplied in the Western Cape, for example, then BEE-style e-cow-nomics told them to seek employment in another province where they were 'under-represented'. On this basis one 'Indian' university human resource director in Durban instructed heads of department not to employ 'Indians' (despite the fact that the KwaZulu-Natal province hosts the largest Indian diaspora in the world). The brown cows were oversupplied and told to seek work in pastures where they were proportionately under-represented.

Structuration of the labour force was complemented by restructuring ownership and control via BEE legislation. BEE requires previously white-owned companies to cede majority shareholdings to what in effect is a very small stratum of recently embourgeoisiefied black partners. Moletsi Mbeki (2009) typifies these new owners as an officially legitimised, poverty-inducing consumptive, rather than a wealth-productive, class fraction. These extractive black cows became protected species, as they are in India.

Transformation cannot be based on growing inequality and crude re-racialisation drawn from past apartheid path dependencies. Separating the population into black, white, brown and coloured cows, and assigning them different economic opportunities is akin to killing the non-racial green pastures that feed them. The South African university has been thus partly 'transformed' from a site of intellectual innovation and original thought to that of servicing clients, markets, political interests and racial quotas. In this scenario, human resources divisions that enforce such quotas have become the ideological state apparatuses holding the academic sector hostage. Post-racialism, the obvious successor to non-racialism, has never been on the new state's agenda.

THE NEW ENTITLEMENT: BLUNDERING ALONG

Educational activist Jonathan Jansen tells students and unemployed graduates in his columns in *The Times* to volunteer, do, get experience, take up unpaid internships to populate their CVs. Waiting for top-paying management posts popped loose by transformation, BEE, affirmative action and racially based equity policies only works for the small politically connected BEE class and less so in a bankrupt and cowed economy that can no longer absorb them. My Law of Mundane Existence reveals that ordinary people have to know how slog when the elite just have to cash their pay cheques, protect their backs and watch out for the Zondo Commission into state capture by adherents of Zupta e-cow-nomics. This is crony capitalism, where the increasingly milked taxpayer mollycoddles the ever-grazing cows.

Economics myths were under scrutiny by the first batch of coursework master's students coterminous with the first election in 1994 that I co-taught. Many refused to study or participate in class. My American colleagues relate a similar experience:

I have some of the worst prepared students ever (I think it's a generational thing because I hear about it from colleagues of other schools). They sit very obediently but don't take any notes. They refuse to read the assignments and show no remorse when they can't answer the most basic questions about them. Their handwriting is so atrocious I can barely read the pathetic verb-less utterances they write. In class, if I ask a question that – I swear – could be answered by a complete stranger on a city bus (eg: What is a problem you see that out-of-control consumerism creates in the US today?), they just say a word with a question mark at the end. 'Taxes?' So I say, 'Well, taxation is not really a problem, is it, because it allows the government to function.' So, another will respond, 'Things?' It goes on and on. I ask them, 'Can you make that a sentence so I can understand what you mean?' And they say, with utter petulance and with great rolling of eyes, something positively nonsensical: 'People think that things are where they could have been!' WHAT?!

I begin to think I'm showing signs of dementia. It is *me*?! Do you get this in South Africa too, or is it just the effects of dreadful public education in the US? HELP!

Whereas in the United States a rapacious capitalism is taken for granted, in South Africa, in 1994, students assured their exasperated lecturers: 'Soon, the ANC will be in government and socialism will provide.' This two-cow conclusion that assumes that 'what's yours is now mine' emerged only after the lecturers had corralled the students in the stifling, locked, seminar room. The class would be allowed to leave only after they explained their otherwise inexplicable refusal to learn. Thirty minutes of excruciating silence had loosened their lips. 'Okay,' I responded, 'now we have a hypothesis to examine.'

My colleague Eric Louw's response was that a contributing factor to the failure of Soviet communism was the myth that 'socialism would provide'. 'Who will pay the taxes for a successful socialism in South Africa?' I asked. The students were astonished that as part of the employed middle class that their own salaries would contribute to the national tax base. They had foolishly assumed that they were lumpen (but salaried) revolutionaries who would be tax-exempt. Indeed, a newly appointed young staffer had complained bitterly that her first payslip reflected a tax deduction. What was I going to do about it, she had demanded.

Why not redistribute Anglo-American's profits, one student asked. A study revealed that if each individual in South Africa were to get an equal share, the income per head in 1994 would be paltry from this then Fortune 500 conglomerate. And so it went, until enlightenment dawned. Socialism is flawed because people venerating passivity want to benefit but not contribute, participate and learn. Resources are finite in this system and grades mean nothing when learning and problem solving are not occurring.

Transformation is not just a matter of signing the register to prove class attendance and paying fees to purchase a certificate. Wealth creation is needed no matter the type of economy. Then, it becomes a question of redistribution. The question is how and under what conditions redistribution (or transformation) can occur.

The class came to a new consciousness because of the discussion. Time is like using cell phones: if it's a question of being 'seen' to be 'doing' even if nothing is being done, we are running on empty. Active participation in a collective learning environment is the key. How do we get there?

TRANSFORMATION IN EDUCATION: RESETTING FROM WHAT TO WHAT?

South Africa was by 1990 facing serious inequalities and economic and educational decay (Serper 2014). Universities were expected, on the one hand, to massify their undergraduate student enrolments, largely with very poor, grievously underprepared students while, on the other hand, they wanted to enhance their international rankings and build research capacity. The contradictions were sharp – this simultaneous expansion of both ill-prepared students and research output was occurring in the face of reduced state subsidies, declining faculty numbers, exhausted and demoralised academics and massive institutional and student debt. Bureaucracies had exploded in size, cost and a new generation of PoW – top management – now earned stratospheric salaries even in the face of widespread student poverty as the previously disadvantaged were enrolled en masse. The excessively high incomes were justified in e-cow-nomic terms by some vice-chancellors and university councils by vaguely referring to them as 'market-related'. But such high pay was only viable by denying other staff salary scales such a mystical market equivalence.

While academics knew what the problem was (no screening, massification, mindless corporatisation, inefficiency, student debt), management blamed academics – the cows – for high failure and dropout rates. When the cost of institutional inefficiency was drawn to management's attention, the Machiavellian retort was that such critics (the cows) were 'resisting transformation' – a kind of sham reasoning that enabled fuglemanship to punish academics for problems not of their own making.

The second law of relevance here is Management by Disorientation. Sourced to Roman General Caius Petronius (AD66), this law has a long lineage:

> We trained hard, but it seemed that every time we were beginning to form up into teams we would be reorganised.

I was later to learn that we tend to meet any new situation by reorganising and for a wonderful method it can be for creating the illusion of progress, while actually producing confusion, inefficiency and demoralisation. (Townsend 1970: 162)

Christopher Merrett was head of administration at the University of KwaZulu-Natal's Pietermaritzburg campus during the time of the merger between Natal and Durban-Westville universities, 2004–2005. In opposing such management by disorientation, and losing his job in the process, his law states, more or less, 'Never let any institutional sector settle and create the impression of transformation by endless (and often fruitless) restructuring.' Restructuring is like being on a treadmill that more often than not goes nowhere – and is a mechanism enabling managerial-led centralisation of power and resources, irrespective of efficiency.

In this regard, Bunk Carter's Law states: 'At any given time there are more important people in the world than important jobs to contain them.' PoW aspirants, in order to secure worthy positions, thus ensure that bureaucracies expand constantly and that work expands to fill the time available. Rarely now do deans, as they once did, lead their faculties from the bottom up. Their responsibilities have been transformed to top-down. They're too busy generating data for Very Important People, or PoWs, who claim to be doing Very Important Jobs, who need to drive Very Posh Cars to deliver on their 'mandates' and who occupy Very Remote Offices, often behind guarded perimeters. Carter's Law comes into play when expanding bureaucracies mutate academics into managers and administrators who are rarely visible anymore to students and faculty except at statutory meetings.

University-wide operating systems are creaking at the seams as even after 'reconfiguration' many of these systems have yet to catch up with the new structures and policies that enabled them. One hour at the coalface is all I asked of our top executives. Become a lecturer, administrator or student for just one day; go undercover if necessary, just like in the reality television show *Undercover Boss*. These shows offer new genres and insights for pop anthropological research – getting down and dirty in Indian textile factories, being trumped by Trump and voted off the set by the survivors. Learn about how the shop floor really works and then you too can experience the daily stresses and frustrations that characterise it. Such experience might also generate some solutions to the problems that academics complain about incessantly.

If we don't get our stress levels under control, we're all going to end up as subjects in the *Spa of Embarrassing Illnesses*, *The Fat Doctor* or similar. This will be our claim to 'good scholarship' – and pandering to the market – as we hyper-individuate, hyper-ventilate and re-interpellate ourselves from being 'good scholars' to experimental subjects/celebrities stripped of any modesty by voyeuristic cameras, or at best, as participant observers, we are pricked and prodded, cut and suctioned, exposed and bared for all the world to see. The difference between 'acting' in these shows and being a social actor in the realm of academementia is that the television contestants can pick up their pay cheques and/or prizes at the door as they leave the studio and go home to normality, possibly feeling better than when they came in. Not only does the world now know what the problem was but also that there is a solution. Not so in academia, where we just go round and round in circles. Once the fat has been suctioned off, we then cut into the muscle, and once that is gone, we are left with skeletons.

But academics do consider deans to be doing Very Important Jobs even as they whiz about in their Very Posh Cars and isolate themselves in their Very Remote Offices. The problem is that with the restructured supposedly neoliberal inversion of 'transformed' responsibility, deans are rarely in the trenches with academics, students, protesting mobs, tear gas and classrooms. Deans have been transformed into suits, caught in a structurational glare that locates them as glaze-eyed flak catchers who are solely responsible to the PoW. Deans, in their own ways, like the rest of us, spend their long and frustrating days putting out fires. Problem is, the fire extinguishers don't work anymore.

Neither does the maths. As one critic lamented: 'This new transformation math has me baffled. What cost-benefit analysis was done to validate mergers? Where are the axioms, and the rules of deduction?' Sherlock Holmes, where are you, other than on television? 'Elementary' was not a term Holmes ever uttered, but little is elementary, or elegantly simple anymore. Policymakers always devise the most complicated solutions to address simple problems.

Budgets are down. Managements resist taking responsibility for ensuring operational efficiency. Yet, performance management (PM) mechanisms assume stable and functioning environments – not characterised by endless glitches, sham reasoning and campuses continuously under siege from arsonists and politicised mobs expecting freebee cows[3]. PM indicators are unable to discount chaos, confusion and operational meltdown, which daily characterise academic working conditions. One university even insisted that processing of PM reports continue by remote means even as COVID-19 had shut down the entire world – a case of literally measuring ourselves to death – the errant self-isolated cows will be counted no matter the crisis.

Where the PoW award themselves bonuses, regardless of their performance, the rest of us have to fiddle our PM scores and the few surviving cows to negotiate the ordeal. Real transformation would enable academics and students to assess their managers' performance in facilitating delivery rather than so often obstructing it.

PoW, or vice-chancellors, are everyone's target, yet the honest ones are trying to clean up the mess. Spare a thought for their stress, the threats levelled against them, the trauma of fire bombings and intimidation. It takes a special breed of South African to do this job. No one has workable solutions, least of all the state that was itself under siege from Zuptanomics during Zuma's kleptocratic presidency.

Earlier, in 1994, the progressives had won the day. That was when the institutions of the new society were put in place. The struggle intensified after 2016 as state and tertiary institutions reasserted themselves, as the previous Zuptanian arch colonists were being brought to account across the new nation. As beneficiaries of both the old and new societies, we all owe our alma maters debts of gratitude. Alumni need to take an interest in the institutions that educated them, to ensure that the task of rebuilding continues and survives the new attacks, to restore the value of public service, and to work with students who want to earn their degrees and make a societal contribution. Alumni have the privilege of hindsight. This is a priceless vantage point and one to be shared with youngsters who have become disillusioned with the contemporary moment, while that small sub-group intent on killing all the cows through the systematic destruction of university campuses compounds the problem.

Rebuilding is a long-term process and we all need to make active contributions. The Organisation for Undoing Tax Abuse, for example, was inaugurated to oppose the outsourcing of our highways to new imperial interests and their bottom-feeding tendrepreneurs who skim contracts by inserting themselves as brokers between service providers, corrupt politicians and state officials. Successive finance ministers have lost their jobs trying to protect the Treasury. South Africa, like societies everywhere in the current conjuncture, is betwixt and between. New corrupt orders are struggling to rise to the surface. Old corrupt orders are digging in. Contestation is the principle of history. This is what is meant by the revolutionary slogan '*A luta continua*' (the struggle continues), though in South Africa, under Zuptanomics, the slogan was more appropriately, 'a loota continua'.

Sometimes, however, like must meet like – farce meets farce. Cold, clinical logic cannot easily explain the 'transformed' institution. The new en-cowed numbers often just do not add up.

Here is why.

Where academics fiddle their key performance areas (KPAs) and dilute the milk, top management applies New Transformation Maths of '1 + 1 = 3'. In such synergetic geometry: two circles partially overlaid on each other results in three forms, even if the middle circle is less circular: 1 + 1 = 3. Alternatively, 1 + 1 means 11 – known as exponential synergy.

So, if you have not seen your glaze-eyed flack catcher recently (because s/he is always in meetings, anxiously tracking enrolment graphs, trying to reach targets, or being (ad)dressed down or up by top management, avoiding contact, exhausted, driving between campuses, at strategic planning retreats, or trying to comprehend transformation maths, and so on), we should apply synergetic principles. If we can synergise two deans into three, we can position the third dean with us in the trenches (which were once lush pastures). Then, using the same principles we can apply the New Maths (or exponential synergy) to manufacture the necessary funny money known as e-cow-nomics to pay them.

The cyber occult is real world – like the volatile financial markets. The three-part *Zeitgeist*, feature-length conspiratorial documentaries, argue that if all the money listed on the world's computers was withdrawn by its owners on a single day, the paper currency spat out would be only 20 per cent of the total. Similar is the virtuality of stock markets, bonds and other chimerical financial instruments that are simply linked genres of a foolish volatile video game.

Money is an imagined entity. Reserve banks manage imagination, not hard cash. 'The markets' are anthropomorphised. When money is no longer virtual, it will no longer exist. This is one of the few instances where the illusion is real. Economics and accounting textbooks do not discuss this much. As one of my regular correspondents, anthropologist Dave Coplan, elucidated:

Definition of cyberspace: that's where the bank keeps your money.

Hard currency: there is no such thing except gold. Paper money is just an IOU based on government promises and resources that may or may not be kept.

Paper money is only for criminals. (Think of the Watson brothers and the Bosassa cash cow factory [Basson 2019]) and the Saxonwold shebeen when politicians left with bags of cash, as told to the Zondo Commission by the all-seeing official drivers of state vehicles.

Too many critical financial analysts are now in the Zeitgeist machine churning out bland government press releases that have nothing to do with reality as we ordinary folks experience it. How do they live with themselves? Their huge salaries no doubt numb the pain and the electronic occult is to blame. Personal computers and then the Internet killed history – digital natives as occurring in the perceptual present now experience everything. Nothing exists outside the Web. The Web is Truth; it is God, all-knowing. All one has to do is to press buttons and the digital magic will do the rest. Students who can write functional sentences are becoming a rarity. Plagiarism rules. The initial punishment I mete out is for plagiarists to undertake a detailed written analysis of the Turnitin reports and to explain to me in a structured essay the high plagiarism incidence, then to fix their essays, with a resubmission and an apology addressed to the university, the taxpayer and their peers. This task the errant students take more seriously than the actual essays they wrote originally. It works because they know that I will not be fooled and that I am prepared to put in the necessary work not to be fooled by such fools.

For good measure, we should engage the services of mathematician/comedian/pianist/singer Tom Lehrer's New

Maths, where he says:

> 'The important thing is not to get the answer right but to understand what one is doing!'[4]

That's why I require a written analysis of the Turnitin report. Transformation (new e-cow-maths) is required to understand, for example, where all the money that was sloshing about at the University of KwaZulu-Natal in 2012 went – that is, why there was so little of it in 2013 and less during 2014, but more in 2015. As a manager explained – and listen for the Lehrer-type piano rhythm – the 2013 university budget, calculated by something called a resource allocation model (RAM), was based on 2011 under-enrolment data when enrolment and graduation targets were not met. The year 2012 was skipped, it got lost in transformation. But where did RAM 2012 go? Good old Tom explains: 'Addition is commutative', a logical mathematical operation that combines two objects at a time.[5] So, if $1 + 1 = 3$ (years $2011 + 2013$ = budget reduction), the answer, if I understand what I am doing, is that less funding (because we had more in 2012) results in greater synergies – we do more with less because less is more. This is the New Transformation Maths. No one understands it.

Throughout the decade of the 2000s deans remained lost in making sense of transformation/transubstantiation/translation math in the e-cow-nomics environment. In a study of over 100 deans, John Randolph Willis observed that doubling of vacation periods enables deans to work with maximum efficiency. If this is not possible, Father Damian Fandel, Dean at Dallas, formulated two rules for effective administration: Rule 1 – Hide! Rule 2 – If they find you, lie! (Martin 1973: 90).

In a global environment where deans have been often repositioned as bean counters, the FACT frame is pertinent: F(airness) A(ccountability), C(ompromise) and T(ransparency).

This approach locates individuals as ends in themselves rather than solely as means to someone else's output objectives. This is known as the Kantian Imperative. Was this not the intention of the Employment Act of 1997? How come, then, so many feel like slaves to form-filling dictates to enable the continued employment of the expensive PoW?

Notes

1. See http://www.allposters.com/-sp/E-cow-nomics-Posters_i2914414_.htm?ac=true

2. Shebeen, an informal drinking place, which is how the then CEO of Eskom, Brian Molefe, tried to ludicrously explain his presence at his Gupta handlers' mansion, a corrupt relationship that looted this national electricity supply company

3. This form of e-cow-nomics enacted by arsonists who from 2017 annually burned intellectual pastures across the country aimed, charged the University of KwaZulu-Natal's vice-chancellor, to 'turn the clock back – to make corrupt practices, parasitic behaviour and mired systems work for individuals and groups at the expense of [the university's] mission', to 'deflect us from initiating sweeping reforms that will ensure the institution's sustainability and heighten its national and international standing'. Those who long benefited from this inertia were dismayed that the era of 'business as usual' is now over. To offer but one example: 'We recently removed 2 000 individuals who have been "professional students" on three-year degrees for eight years or more, without paying fees and routinely holding the institution ransom through unrest for personal concessions.' The perpetrators of the violence were resisting their loss of opportunities for 'private enrichment; it is a threat to unleash chaos in the face of our successes in pursuit of establishing order and sustainability'. This statement was issued by Nana Poku, in response to the burning of a lecture theatre on 12 March 2020. (https://www.timeslive.co.za/news/south-africa/2020-03-12-ukzn-removes-2000-professional-students-whove-taken-eight-years-to-do-a-three-yearcourse/) But worse, says Njabulo Ndebele (2017), is the burning by students of memory itself

4   Read the lyrics at: https://genius.com/Tom-lehrer-new-math-lyrics

5   See: https://genius.com/Tom-lehrer-new-math-lyrics

3 The Backlog Syndrome

'Who's going to answer the phones?' was the plaintive cry of a senior professor as the cost-saving realities of school reconfiguration kicked in during the 2000s. Universities calculate the monetary cost of an employee but not the symbolic benefit an employee brings. One known rationale for restructuring is that academics could be relieved of the burden of ever-increasing, distracting, time- and research-killing daily administration. This reversal is a variation of Alfred Sloan's Organisational Syndrome: 'Since no-one can prove where efficiencies lie in an organisation there is no objective basis for the allocation of new investment' (Sloan 1967: 48; see also Martin 1973: 37). This leads to Charles Reich's Law of Hierarchical Reality:

> Top executives know only what they are told. In effect, they are 'briefed' by others, and the briefing is both limiting and highly selective. The executive is far too busy to find out very much for himself ... the briefing may be three steps removed from the facts, and thus be interpretation built upon interpretation – nearer fiction than fact by the time it reaches the man at the top. (Reich 1970)

The cry about who now answers the phones reminds me of the exasperated editor of a French academic journal with whom I was working in the early 1980s: 'Why do you Africans always blame the West for your woes, just do answer the mail and the West will respond positively!' This Never Answer the Letter Law (Martin 1973: 86) took on a new form when voicemail was introduced in the 1990s. Academics mostly used this facility to shield themselves from incessant incoming calls when secretaries' hours were summarily cut. In the early 1990s, no one answered the phones at Luthuli House and African National Congress (ANC) came to stand for 'Answer No Calls', as the ANC's Mewa Ramgobin told me.

OF PAPER, UNCOMPLETION QUOTIENTS AND WORKLOADS

'Too much damn paperwork.' This was my A-rated colleague's observation on having to sit through an interminable meeting on research centres. 'How does anyone get any real work done?' he asked me. The 75-year-old Bill Harris was delighted that he would retire soon – no more paperwork. The paperwork, of course, is now electronic, with no storage or budgetary limits. Whole university divisions have been established simply to extract data from all of us. Though now drowning in data, the information is useless because there is too much of it and nobody really knows what to do with it. So managers just ask for more and more of it, thereby securing their jobs. Strangely, often they do not know where it is or how to access it. Therefore, they recurrently require the academics to regenerate the same data, often on different forms and in different templates, which are continuously revised, rendering previous data irrelevant. The Fitzhugh Phenomenon best articulates this condition:

> Everybody is somewhat responsible for everything and nobody is completely responsible for anything. So there's no way of assuming authority, or accountability … [employees] spend all their time coordinating with each other and shuffling paper [now emails] back and forth, and that's what causes all the red tape and big staffs … nobody can do anything without checking with seven other people. (cited in Martin 1973: 42)

As philosopher John Collier put it in an email circulated to academics at the University of KwaZulu-Natal: 'Linear-minded quality control procedures hide lateral incompetence.'

One head of school told his staff to keep correspondence to just four lines, failing which, he did not have time to read it, let alone act on it. Therefore, what we get now are templates. Templates feed Charles Vail's axioms of hierarchiology. Vail, once a university vice-president, was the first to study the bureaucracy. Vail's Axiom 1 reads: 'Work seeks the lowest level', but increasingly at universities work seeks a higher level where heads of departments now do the tasks once done by secretaries. Vail's Axiom 2: 'The percentage of work at any level of the hierarchy that remains undone is invariant, which is why bureaucracies expand ad infinitum' (see Martin 1973: 48–50). Corollary 2 is relevant here: 'The amount of material to be filed increases in proportion to the amount already filed', which then reactivates Axiom 1. The bureaucracy is unable to locate, connect or process the information already filed with it by academics now also doing basic administration jobs.

Bureaucracies are inhabited by two kinds of people: (i) The Abominable No Man prevents solutions, while (ii) the Willingman gets things done by taking responsibility and evading decideophobia (Parkinson, cited in Martin 1973: 76). Traditionally, managers were the Willingman leaders, while administrators were the decision-avoiders. However, under managerialism, neither makes decisions as these are cascaded from the People of Worth (PoW) as non-negotiable. To paraphrase T.L. Martin (1973: 38–39), often, when academics are promoted and acquire more power they become progressively less sure of what needs to be done. Those who have no authority, however, do know what needs to be done but as they rise through the ranks, they lose this awareness. This is Matsch's Maxim: 'A fool in a high station is like a man at the top of a mountain – everything appears small to him and he appears small to everybody' (cited in Martin 1973: 40).

The circularity that results from Vail's axioms creates the Backlog Syndrome that ensures that work is never completed. If we do not have a backlog, we cannot make claim to continued employment. Therefore, the bureaucrats devolve their backlogs to the academics where the buck stops, mainly because heads of departments increasingly lack a natural lower (secretarial) level to which to devolve their backlogs. The highest uncompletion quotient in any institution is to be therefore found in the higher ranks. Thus was management science born. I wonder how many still teach Northcote Parkinson's Theory of Hierarchiology? In this context, Corollary 2 of his First Law states that 'Officials make work for each other.' They also make work for everyone else and hijack time that was previously available for productive activities.

Though classroom lecturers work in terms of quarterly and annual cycles, researchers do not. These are linked to what is feasible during specific phases of the research, in light of time, funding and non-tangible resources, and are dependent on external factors (like pandemics and natural disasters, student protests and resulting campus closures) that cannot always be anticipated. Measuring output that does not include preparation, and rejected or under-review publications, on an annual basis is thus ill advised. Research is reliant on a series of considerations that emerge out of the projects themselves. Therefore, I have called on Vail's Axiom 2 and included in my own performance management (PM) form my backlog: stuff I am still thinking about, half-done articles, writing newspaper columns, wasting time at conferences and webinars during the COVID-19 lockdown, doing peer reviews, community engagement, footling around in the field, ruminating and talking to my peers.

Since the PM industry took Parkinson seriously as a model for effective operation, instead of detecting his subversive irony, I have entered the filling in of my PM form on the form itself. Now, I have allocated a percentage to the amount of time consumed in this form-filling exercise, which simultaneously addresses the Vail and Parkinson principles of how best to keep ever-expanding bureaucracies busy. As more staff are appointed, more work is undone and so more people must be brought in to do it. But this does not axiomatically apply in the academic sector where fewer and fewer academic staff do more and more work in less and less time. Even as the stress builds, and the working day stretches into sixteen hours, in one instance I know of, a professor received a warning from his dean for taking time off to consult his doctor. The transgression: he did not pre-apply for half a day's sick leave!

Performance management is being questioned in the business world. One CEO of a listed company observed that a remuneration process driven by key performance indicators is mechanistic and often results in dysfunctional behaviour and unintended consequences. If a CEO is told to meet metric-like earnings per share, s/he's incentivised to get only that result – even at the expense of the firm's long-term future.[1] South African universities have the same attitude to publication and, increasingly, citation metrics – these narrow results tend to trump other necessary duties.

One of my most appreciative readers, Mohomed Haffajee, formerly of the University of KwaZulu-Natal sent me this response on PM:

> Filling out our SAPSE [South African Post-Secondary Education] forms annually entailed analysing how we spent 100% of our time at university. I was convinced that the university bundled them up for each faculty, sent it off to some dark underground bureaucratic chamber with a big padlock in Pretoria (God knows where) and then threw them all in there to slowly oxidise into brown toilet paper. To test my hunch I decided to send the same figures on my SAPSE forms for three successive years in a row to see if it mattered. It didn't. I understand exactly what you mean, except it now gets stored in some massive green matrix for non-earthlings to try to figure if there's intelligent life on earth.

My objective in developing this uncompletion quotient thesis is to develop a huge backlog and to be employed until I am 80. I will then bequeath my backlog to my successor and wait for my articles in the pipeline to appear over the next ten years. She or he can then fill in the forms and claim my incentives on my behalf. Paper still rules – even if it is now intangible.

Universities, like algebra, should be about relationships, propositions and possibilities. Knowledges, especially indigenous knowledges, exist in the collective rather than the individual mind; they resist the tourniquet of monetisation and cost-to-company calculations. DNA sequencing may never have been discovered had the scientists involved been told by the PoW to earn their keep through the spreadsheet economy. Brutal instrumentalism heralds the death for humankind. As Vladimir Lenin once remarked, the capitalist will happily sell the rope to his executioner. Similarly, the educational bureaucrat now auditing the tertiary sector via profit and loss statements, as at Texas A&M University and increasingly in South Africa, will claim fiscal accountability at the very moment that there is nothing left to be accounted for. Many students already assume this state of entropy – education is nothing more than a service, whether paid for or not.

One cannot just check out of Hotel Academentia, whether one is in the United States or South Africa. The catharsis of storytelling is the only respite offered.

EDUCATORS, FORDISM AND EXHAUSTION

'I'm taking early retirement because I want to teach. Can't stand educational Fordism.' Fordism was on the march in the tertiary sector 100 years after Henry Ford had created a conveyer belt production line to churn out Model T cars. That is when homogenisation started. 'You can have any colour as long as it is black,' he preened. Educational Fordism arrived in South Africa in the late 1990s, trading as first 'efficiency' and then as 'transformation'. The two discourses merged and when the cows questioned the resulting corporatisation, this was dismissed by the PoW as 'resisting transformation' and therefore deemed by many new cow-herders to be racist. The implied racism was emphasised after 2016 when transformation became 'decolonisation' – with which everyone is compelled to comply.

My colleague's complaint about the education production line, made while he and I were taking a leak in a men's room, reminded me of the astonishment that usually greeted my public lectures in the United States during the 1980s. These always drew forth the question: 'How is it that your university allows you to be so radical?' My response was that the four anti-apartheid liberal universities were, to greater or lesser extent, democratic beacons in a neo-fascist ocean: 'We elect our deans and if they don't address our concerns then we can unelect them.' During the deafening response from my American audiences, they raged on about their own obstructive deans in a society that claimed to be the model of democracy globally.

Prior to 2000, deans at the four South African liberal English-language universities represented their constituents (academics), on whose behalf they worked and to whom they were accountable. A reversal then occurred. Many do try to balance between inexorable top-down, bottom-up pressures, but this is the surest way to burn out. An analogy is the newspaper industry, corporatised in the early 1990s. Editors working for Independent Newspapers, under the new Irish owner, now found themselves accountable to their marketing and subscription departments, their editorial autonomy compromised (Dasnois and Whitfield 2019: 41–42). Some left the profession in protest to more conducive environments.

Managers and administrators outnumber academics at many institutions. The only way I could discuss this asymmetrical ratio without being fired was not to ask. Thus I referred to a naughty tautology written on a bowl that I had when a student:

> Why do rabbits have more fun than people?
> Because there are more rabbits.
> Why are there more rabbits?
> Because rabbits have more fun than people.

To extrapolate:

> Maybe the managers have more fun than academics?
> They reproduce faster – bureaucratically, that is.
> Why do they reproduce faster?
> Because there are more managers.
> Why do academics no longer have any fun?
> Because the managers have taken the fun out of the academy.

How does one measure performance when one is chasing rabbits? Lionel Posthumus, a dean at the University of Johannesburg, responded to my rabbit analogy: 'This is shockingly true! You have to chase rabbits as they jump out of the holes and chase them until a new rabbit appears which will take you in an opposite direction. If universities had to be self-sustainable they would not last beyond a couple of years!'

The flipside is Barzun's Lament, which says: 'Education is a passion and a paradox. Millions want it and commend it, at the same time they are willing to degrade it by trying to get it free of charge and free of work' (cited in Martin 1973: 116). This is the result of transformation: open admissions, free marks, grade inflation, the entitlement discourse of 'pass one, pass all', the recasting of students as clients and the popular assumption that institutions can afford to accept everybody and that universities should provide social welfare and allocate their residences to address the national housing shortage.

My advice to my men's room friend was to take the package, go out and educate, be synergistic and teach the masses how to multiply (that is, do Maths). Remake democracy in different spheres. Transformation must be linked to democratisation.

OF PASSING AND FAILING

'Pass one, pass all' was the opportunistic catchphrase of the 1990s, uttered by militant students who claimed that administrative justice was thus best served. The ranking of class essays from good to bad was considered undemocratic and demands were made for marks to be homogenised across the whole class. Some students would even threaten lecturers – 'We know where you live' – while the more polite two-cow-inclined students would try to negotiate higher marks on the basis of racial congruity with their lecturers – 'Let's make a deal, black-on-black'. Then, there were those weak students who 'knew' that they deserved an A and tried to negotiate an upgrade by camping in departments (sometimes with a parent) for days on end, trying to exhaust the patience and sanity of their tutors.

No one thought that he or she should fail for any reason at all. One ingenious master's student told me that the text that he had plagiarised from the Web, which he had laboriously copied in longhand, in fact was plagiarised by the Web author from his own handwritten essay. Our hardworking international African students and lecturers looked on with a combination of horror, bemusement and disbelief. The conveyer belt that relied on 'pass one, pass all' was a national industry.

My response to 'Pass one, pass all' was 'Fail one, fail all'. I would then ask whether the student who had failed would fly with a pilot with a condoned pass. Until recently, this had been a hypothetical question. A graphic reminder of what happens when we pass students who should fail occurred in Taiwan when a pilot, who had failed his simulator test, crashed his plane, killing everyone on board. One of the engines had cut out. Instead of switching it on again, he stupidly switched off the engine that was running, which might have righted the plane.[2]

Then there are those pilots who have failed their psychology assessments who have committed suicide-by-plane, killing hundreds of their passengers. On top of these failed pilots are their failed managers, as at Malaysia Airlines who kept their planes flying over the Ukrainian war zone – with predictable results. The managers who fail to manage their pilots and plane routes can kill. One parent wrote to me of his son doing electrical engineering: 'Don't be surprised when engineers shock themselves to death.' Professors in one medical school ask, 'Would you knowingly consult a surgeon with a 50 per cent pass?'

I have refused to approve doctorate theses that arrive on my desk looking like badly formatted incoherent technical reports. No matter, their home institutions accept them anyway because, I am told, the other examiners' assessments were positive. The bar for entry requirements is often set so low for both staff and students that promotion of students to the next level is the only way to meet the unrealistic targets set by management, as they try to leverage state subsidy that is based on throughput.

Working with a team of Australian child psychologists on over-imitation and technical problem solving among Aboriginal, Kalahari and urban pre-schoolers in the two countries, I have learnt that, historically, indigenous children were treated as adults by their parents, learning through apprenticeship rather than via formal educational strategies that separate them from each other for most of the day. The latter is the Cartesian, industrial way. Astonishingly, our own conditions of service do not recognise the implications of this, even if babies and children are sometimes in the classrooms along with their parents and other adults. Unlike the children of traditional indigenous communities who learn on the job, and who pay the price when a mistake is made, many students in the formal education system simply learn how to buck the system, irrespective of adult guidance.

Hence, my proactive philosophy is that 'Fail one, fail all' will *save* thousands of lives, whereas 'Pass one, pass all' will *kill* thousands.

Just think of all those minibus drivers with forged licenses who kill their passengers by the dozen because they think that physical laws and the rules of the road do not apply to them. They think that they can pass one, pass all, usually on the wrong side of the road and in the emergency lanes. Since just about everyone has contempt for the rules of the road, Arrive Alive should just close shop and leave it to motorists to 'kill one, kill all'. Thanks to COVID-19 and the lockdown, very few accidents occurred over Easter 2020.

The problem with the strategy of making the country ungovernable during the late 1980s, with its associated discourse of 'freedom now, education later', is that education got lost in translation. Education became associated with chaos and mediocrity was popularly certified as democratic.

I am not ready to fly with failed pilots. As was pointed out by my colleague Dewey Du, a Chinese translation scholar:

> To me 'pass one, pass all' simply does not make sense. There must have been some consequence of it? One of the students I taught now became a high school teacher. Now she was complaining to me about how different her students were from those in high school 10 years ago. They were not willing to learn anything or do any work (because they do not feel the need to), paid less respect to teachers, cheat in exams. People easily get influenced when the news, the adults, the government, the whole population now focus on cheating and making easy money to be 'successful'. For the case of 'pass one, pass all', democracy means sameness and get-together while different marks means unfairness and prejudice.

Academentia is everywhere.

DEATH BY FORMS

Some think that academics teach. Research, we know, is what we do after hours when we are not 'working'. This synergy applies even though the workload spreadsheet is calculated on a 40-hour week – that is, academics work for 'free' after hours as there is no way of calculating this extra labour into workload reporting mechanisms.

What South African lecturers really do is fill in forms: purchasing, registration, publication outputs, student throughputs, key performance indicators, research evaluations, workload calculations, enrolment entries, mark lists, class registers, student risk assessments, funds raised, ticking 'decolonisation' indices, Department of Higher Education and Training (DHET) claims and, soon, how much toilet paper we consume. Few university systems talk to each other, which means that the same information has to be constantly regenerated manually under different categories to cross-populate all of the systems. The only consistency is disorientation by upgrading to yet more flawed software. Mistakes wrought by fuglemanship occur under these conditions.

The transformed corporate university now has multiple layers of (mis)management and each kludgeman, exemplars of Peter's Principle and the Final Placement Syndrome, creates work for the level below, to the extent that students, who are the majority, are often invisible – except for the noise they make.

The story of the University of KwaZulu-Natal's unique merger, one among many, is an important one that illustrates kludgemanship, on the one hand, and e-cow-nomics, on the other. Documented in two books, each seemingly written in opposition to the other, Malegapuru Makgoba and John Mubangizi's (2010) compilation offers a structuration perspective, one that pits management against the cows: academics, support and administrative staff. Students, unions, alumni and the public were not included in this anthology. Nithaya Chetty and Christopher Merrett's (2014) counter-narrative reads like a thriller, revealing how, when faced with communication restrictions, coercive management and harassment-by-court action, academics will always find subversive channels to discuss and do things that infuriate the fuglemans. When read in conjunction, the two books offer an instructive dialectical narrative of how different constituencies perceived the conditions, tensions and conflicts during the period of the merger (2004–2008). Transformation for management was couched in neoliberal assumptions, discursively cloaked in an essentialist black economic empowerment (BEE) Africanist discourse. For academics and support staff, transformation was lost as a result of over-structuration at the expense of individuals who inhabited the increasingly oppressive and rigid structures. This resulted in an autocracy governed by punitive hierarchiology that dehumanised staff and constituted them as errant factory workers. Ultimately, what gives is sustained interest by lecturers in participating in institutional governance.

The struggles at the University of KwaZulu-Natal bear an uncanny resemblance to the much more traumatic national tales told by Alide Dasnois and Chris Whitfield (2019) after 2015 at Independent Newspapers. Their experience occurred when a new autocratic and self-serving owner claiming struggle credentials took ownership and control and systematically traumatised, fired, pushed out, belittled and threatened legal action against staff alleged to be resisting transformation. This discourse and its associated practices were created to foster a national moral panic in multiple sectors to enable Zuma-supporting fractions within the new elite to capture institutions and to recreate them in their own image. One difference with the University of KwaZulu-Natal, however, was that cleaners, lecturers and deans forcefully voiced their concerns to an upper management itself riven with internal feuding (see Tomaselli and Caldwell 2019). The procedures, practices and discourses that were applied across the country were similar. At Gupta/Zupta TV and

The New Age, Rajesh Sundaram (2018), a senior broadcast journalist imported from India in violation of visa requirements, revealed how these channels were designed to loot state coffers of advertising funding. Of a totally different order is the utterly harrowing story of terror tactics taken against the 'SABC 8'. Eight broadcast journalists had opposed the brutal censorship regime and newsroom capture imposed by its then megalomaniacal chief operating officer, Hlaudi Motsoeneng (Krige 2019). In this instance, death threats, physical intimidation and the death of one of the eight was a tragic consequence of manic transformation that had no goal other than the expression of one individual's ego, whose reign of terror served Zuptanomics well. Other studies on state capture and on how whole cities have been stolen by the Zuptanites include Crispian Olver (2017); Pieter-Louis Myburgh (2017, 2019); James-Brent Styan and Paul Vecchiatto (2019); Styan (2015); Thandeka Gqubule (2017) and Jacques Pauw (2017), among many others.

Universities were not exempt from similar processes but these were less concealed because of the more open nature of the academic public sphere.

UBUNTU

Universities are supposed to function as scholarly communities. However, when I hear comments emanating from managers such as 'Turkeys don't get to choose at Christmas', I get the chills. This response to a staff member who had queried restructuring from above is an inversion of the Kantian imperative. What is left is a soulless institution on life support, measured by output indicators, auditing software and adversarial communication practices that fly in the face of sensible management theory.

'African values' and ubuntu (communitarianism) are recurring exhortations in the post-apartheid era, as is the paradigm of indigenous knowledge systems. These discourses assume the collective as the basis for decision-making, repository of knowledge and social interaction. The idea of collegiality recognises the collective characteristics of indigenous knowledge systems and the integration of community and individual. Why is it then that the practice of collegiality was in such short supply and seen by some as an imperialist Western racism (Makgoba and Chetty 2010: 157)?

The loss of collegiality, indeed its repression by the institution, is one of the outcomes of corporatised transformation. In my mixed metaphor, collective slaughter of the Christmas turkeys perhaps is the most efficient way of getting the product (milk in my cow analogy) to the consumer. Is the modern massified university factory just too complex to function otherwise? The lack of institutional soul does not excuse individual (mis)behaviour, however. Reciprocation and exchange in some quarters is considered a sign of weakness. These are not behaviours caused by structure or policy. They are enacted by individuals, who use the institution for their own personal benefit.

Can the humanities arrest this corporate drift? That is the subject of the next chapter.

Notes

1. *Financial Mail*, 12 January 2017: 5
2. Read more at: http://www.cbc.ca/news/world/taiwan-plane-crash-pilot-pulled-wrong-throttle-shut-down-engine-1.3135213

4 Of Science and Souls

'The Future of the Humanities' was the name of an Academy of Science of South Africa (ASSAf) panel on which I served in the late 2000s (see ASSAf 2011). Quite why scientists wanted non-scientists to write a report for a science academy on disciplines that are not hard sciences was, initially, a mystery. Intriguingly, it was a mystery worth investigating.

The humanities are in trouble: declining enrolments, smaller departments closing, huge staff-to-student ratios in others and parental suspicion. Students who are rejected from the sciences and commerce end up in the leaky sink that the humanities have become.

The humanities are the 'soul' of the university. The display banners that frame inaugural lectures and graduation ceremonies in imposing auditoriums tell us this. This refrain often also occurs at faculty meetings when the asymmetrical distribution of resources that favour the sciences are lamented by the impoverished humanities lecturers. Television dramas often reveal that criminal lawyers lack souls. But what of science and scientists? Richard Dawkins (2006) talks about the 'God delusion'. Can he be correct when the academy itself arose in the Middle Ages out of European theological institutions? Is this the soul that the humanities are trying to resuscitate? Are the humanities hovering in the night of the living dead, like a ghastly Depression-era Hollywood B horror movie?

Where social science counts phenomena, the humanities creatively describe and explain them, looking for inner meaning. Like our lost souls, the ASSAf panel searched for an appropriate definition. 'Close readings', suggested one wag, who described the motley bunch of anthropologists, sociologists, political scientists, educationists and literary scholars as 'general dealers'. Dig below the surface of this dealership and one finds among this bunch a lapsed botanist, a one-time mathematician and a partly erstwhile urban geographer turned media scholar. Conceptual hybridity characterises the humanities, suggested a transdisciplinary apostle. A third located the genesis of the humanities as the last gate in the defence of civilisation as we know it. Civilisation has been, of course, its own worst enemy for thousands of years. The barbarians are often in control (cf. Zuptanomics).

What is a close reading?[1] I dealt with this phrase all the time as chair of my school's Higher Degree Committee. For me, more social scientist than litterateur, this is a meaningless term, unless made specific. How will the 'close reading' occur? What methods will be applied to assessing what? Conversely, being human cannot be encapsulated in the relative crudity offered by number crunching. Being human requires a soul – and a soul requires the study of meaning, how meaning is made, interpreted and acted on. In other words, what is the meaning of meaning? This takes us into the realm of semiotics, mathematics, physics and even metaphysics; indeed, all disciplines are concerned with making, explaining and applying meaning. This is what, as physicist Derek Wang told our students, is meant by his conclusion that science is a cultural expression. If this is so, different cultures express different conceptions of science even if the practice of science is the single constant.

Once an implacably positivist geography student, I remember my class, well-schooled in positivism, responding with derision to the argument by Richard Hartshorne (1959) that the practice of geography is partly intuitive and, therefore, beyond the rigours of science. That which was scientific could be measured and was legitimate, while that which could not be counted was consigned to the realm of 'the beyond'. The academy largely rejects that which is to be found in this unknowable realm, defined by philosopher Immanuel Kant (1998) as the noumenal. Much of my work as a documentary film-maker and cultural researcher, however, has tried to explain the unexplainable. Do noumenal occurrences fall into the realm of anthropology? Theology? Indigenous knowledge systems? Cosmology? Literature? How do these disciplines help us make meaning of the meaning that non-scientists (and ordinary people) mean?

The recognition of different ontologies, different frames of reference, different cosmologies in the era of postmodernism (and of decolonising) has recovered the legitimacy of that which is unexplainable, or still to be explained. Religion remains the blind spot of most disciplines (as in the Dawkins book) (see Eagleton 2006), but – like the principle of resistance – it has always underpinned one of the key forces of history.

Corporatisation and bureaucracy always puts soul under pressure as the structure, not people, determines meaning. Structures are managed in specific ways meaningful to the managers, but those ways may lack a sense of what it means to be human. It is then up to the managers and those being managed to invest meaning in practice and to keep the values of participation, ubuntu and humanitarianism in close view (close readings may be required!). Structuration is also a cultural expression – if a soulless one, as Nithaya Chetty and Christopher Merrett (2014) concluded with regard to 'transformation' at the University of KwaZulu-Natal. Unlike the *X-Files* motto, the truth it not 'out there', it's in here.

Ubuntu starts with small actions like respect for the individual within the framework of the community – academocracy.

HUMANITIES TO THE RESCUE

While the humanities everywhere are under threat, the national South African horizon has changed dramatically in recent years (see Frassinelli 2020).

The ASSAf Consensus Panel on the future of the humanities laid out the actual philosophical groundwork by addressing conceptual, employment and related issues (2011). Simultaneously, the Charter for the Humanities, a different coterminous initiative, recommended reorganisation, which resulted in the establishment of the National Institute for Humanities in 2015 by the then minister of the Department of Higher Education and Training (DHET), Blade Nzimande.[2]

Humanities scholars think of themselves as the last bulwark, the critical cut, against capitulation to socially alienating, neoliberal, technicist, ahistorical and two-cow economistic imperatives. The humanistic high ground aims to protect the practice of critique, the political dialectic, the critical cut and thus democracy itself. As the word 'humanities' suggests, critique should recognise that it is people (who feel, hope, love and fear) who occupy instrumentalist structures created by often alienating regulation and governance. The idea that (all) individuals – not just the People of Worth (PoW) – are ends in themselves is often lost in transformation/translation/transubstantiation.

Where the Charter speaks to policymakers and institutions, the ASSAf study addressed student, parent, employer and humanities lecturer concerns. The Charter's open-ended approach tactically located Africa in the world. Its planning was in the detail, but the budgeting was in the realm of (a perhaps welcome) idealism that is testing the imperatives that are, ironically, pushing the academy in the opposite direction – towards instrumentalism, managerialism and massification. Some universities, in their relentless march towards instrumentalism, proposed that their 'teaching' staff earn education diplomas. They will be taught how to teach the taught and how to tighten the tautology that what research-led universities do is teach banking – education style. The good news is that the researchers who wish to critically educate their charges, rather than shovel pre-primed information down students' throats will resist, though bureaucrats who have boxes to tick will punish them. Will the technocrats who push technocratic creep be made to obtain education diplomas to learn what it is academics supposedly do, putting education and ability to THINK above mechanistic training? Don't bank on it.

En route to campus I pass a B&B sporting the sign, 'Guests wanted. No experience necessary.' This catchy blurb could well be a metaphor for university admission policies. While we all know that many undergraduates are nearly illiterate, the new strategic plan that imposes admission 'targets' on already straining institutions, has now ensured that many of our honours students are just as underprepared. 'Students wanted. No experience necessary' seems to be the mantra. In contrast, the private Independent Institute of Education advertised more sensibly: 'Thinkers Wanted – not for everyone.'[3]

Similarly, I am one of those unrehabilitated (humanist) Marxists who accept that universities are elitist institutions. Only the obviously literate should be admitted. How else would we do research and reproduce ourselves? Illiterates cannot read Karl Marx, but they certainly can get the wrong end of his stick, possibly wrecking entire nations as a result.

The annual enrolment target tactic simply means that more and more students need more and more remedial teaching, more and more attention and more and more counselling. This creates more and more administration and results in less and less research and reading time. The targets allocated to faculties and schools twinned with this process are little more than the filling up of lifeboats with the bewildered who don't know how to steer them, let alone find stable ground. Until we find our bearings, there is nowhere to go except to contemplate what to do with the deckchairs on the *Costa Concordia* (where the captain, unlike on *The Titanic*, was the first to abandon ship).

With campuses tilting with all the illiterates huddled near the lifeboats, what is the solution? Robert L. Saunders's First Law of Educational Innovation holds that 'faculty opposition will stifle innovation and developments' (cited in Martin 1973: 99). The remedy is to ensure that senior academics at least are literate by insisting that they have PhDs – or convincing impressions thereof. The overall effect is a variation of the Weber-Fechner Law manifested in the You-Have-To-Run-Faster-To-Stand-Still Syndrome (cited in Martin 1973: 98). What this law, derived from physics, means is that thanks to top management action to produce another perceptible change it is necessary to produce a force that is stronger than any already present. This means that senior appointments with PhDs will outweigh the many illiterates who occupy our classrooms. The question now is how to ensure that the PhDs held by staff are evidence of literacy?

However, when I read the often incomprehensible communiqués from human resources on when accumulative and other forms of leave apply, I feel illiterate. Making sense of instrumentalism in an educational environment unsuited to the endless categorisation of our activities, time and courses renders us illiterate, subjected as we are to management assumptions that are mismatched with academics' activities. Perhaps, this is the postmodern condition. The categories that govern academics reassure the bureaucrats in the Administration Block while strangling academics in red tape. How else can institutions persuade all academics to do their jobs? A few still give truth to the myth that all academics only work at their own leisure.[4] Often, this unproductive cohort is the reason why management-by-numbers is now the norm.

Writing and reading postmodern theory requires sophisticated literacy, but when students opportunistically claim postmodernism, in some cases, some supervisors require no experience. Such students who are failed by other, literate, professors, then complain that their erratic expression and presentation, confused grammar and SMS spelling, and idiotic referencing is actually encouraged by (postmodern) lecturers. No wonder the bureaucrats are bureaucratic. Theirs is the only way to make sense of a world waddling in its own twaddle.

The new bureaucratic lingo assigned me as 'research leader' in my school. Shades of North Korea? I wondered whether my students should have addressed me as 'Dear Leader'? The Humanities Charter, however, unlike North Korea, aims to elevate our institutions into the global arena in which Africans will begin to think of their futures, and not just take refuge in path dependencies of the 'imagined past'. The Charter and the ASSAf report, when read together, provide both the analysis and the strategy.

Those of us in the humanities often feel like orphans, the marginalised and the forgotten. Scientists, engineers and mathematicians in resource meetings, scorned the arts because our students earned less state subsidy. And we were scoffed at because we tended to be barefoot and wore tatty T-shirts. When students trashed the campus during the early 1990s, a courageous dean of arts would remark in Senate that the students had good organisational skills. We were not the best self-promoters in those days.

The ASSAf panel learned that humanities graduates do get jobs; indeed, they eventually get jobs in the sectors in which they want to work. Not only that, they are hugely self-reliant, more often than not they work as consultants, being their own bosses. Humanities graduates earn less than engineers but they are greatly appreciated by scientists and engineers, as attested to in their invitations to ASSAf membership and the fact that ASSAf recommended the institutionalisation of the humanities within national science policy.

The DHET Charter attracted sustained national media exposure. The significance of the unpublicised ASSAf report is that it dismisses popular myths that denigrate a humanities degree vis-à-vis employment prospects. Significantly, the Charter fractures the common-sense notion derived from the Berlin Conference of 'Africa' in 1878 as a homogeneous, isolated entity. It calls for recognition of the full spectrum of research output, including books, and better staff-student ratios.

A NEW IMAGINARY

As 'complex systems of presumption', imaginaries consist of 'patterns of forgetfulness and attentiveness' (Vogler 2002: 625) that build 'upon implicit understandings' that underpin and enable common practices (Gaonkar 2002: 4). European Enlightenment philosophy and libertarianism that prevailed during the 1980s and 1990s was considered alienating and anti-transformational by some sections of the new bureaucratic class, which nevertheless took its cue from neoliberalism, after the university mergers from 2004 onwards. Thus was a new structuration devised to re-imagine institutions to relocate them into a new 'transformed' order. Legacy and alternative imaginaries were 'corrected'.

The post-Cold War, Western, post-apartheid, neoliberal conjuncture reshaped academia as a new site for commodity relations. To be socially transformative, however, all paradigms need to recover position, rights, critique, dialectical engagement and social justice. The hegemony of 'data' and auditing needs to be ruptured and rethought and universities should enable 'unruly' pedagogies' (Bethlehem and Harris 2012). To be 'unruly' is to defamiliarise the familiar, to disrupt taken-for-granteds. A new unruly paradigm would be relevant, proactive and acquisitive. This transformative imaginary would:

- be all-inclusive, generating employable (critical) graduates. Authority (with a small 'a') should enable the citizenry (the aca-democracy) rather than reside solely in Textuality, Authority/Bureaucracy/Hierarchiology or fuglemanship;
- engage with critical and indigenous methodologies and invest analysis with new, diverse, pluralistic ways of doing and making sense;
- equip graduates with expertise to successfully manoeuvre within institutions for career purposes. This practice

would take into account the plurality of ontologies and identities that now jostle for legitimation and power in a postmodern, pluralistic world where an anti-diversity trend and xenophobia, especially in South Africa, has nevertheless begun to emerge; and

- replace the idea that students are 'clients' and question accounting practices such as assessing an academic's cost-to-company that commoditise academic practices. Audits would highlight contribution to society.

What is to be protected is not Eurocentrism or Afrocentrism or abstract notions of civilisation and hegemony of the canonical Text (often argued to be the repository of civilisation, or social theory that claims universal application). Rather, the new transformative imaginary requires that instead of defending paradigm fundamentalism and Western civilisation (and its philosophy made possible by the Enlightenment), we rather critically engage this corpus to build dynamic humanities that respond to the myriad contexts in which the diversity of multicultural generations now find themselves.

THE NATION, TRANSFORMATION AND IMAGINARIES

As with the humanities and 'transformation', Benedict Anderson (1983: 47) similarly argues that 'the nation' is an abstraction. Nation is a construct of the imagination. Nation imagines a community that is both sovereign and limited, to be engineered through re-structuration, discursively described as 'transformation' and implemented through legislation and coercion, presented as the necessary, natural and the right thing to do. The imperative to create a transformed image of the nation arises mostly during periods of distinct social stress: when new internal developments, or external pressures, undermine a sense of continuity, when most strikingly, there is a 'need for "ethnic revival"' (Smith 1986: 176).

Having transited from apartheid, 'transformation' quite soon lost its broader inclusive and democratising objective and as 'an all-purpose word of justification, slipped into buttressing many specific ANC [African National Congress] goals such as the need for party members to occupy all significant state offices' (Johnston 2014: 175). Overzealous partisan/racial interpretation resulted in social fracturing as the new rulers applied it as a form of racial manifest destiny – Authority – with the intention of monopolising nation building. To question, even on the basis of principle, the authority of the president, vice-chancellors, deans, heads of department and line managers generally, was often seen by the new elite and university PoW to be opposing transformation, denying reconciliation or just being plain racist. Transformation in this sense was never meant to be democratic; it was instituted Soviet-style to serve the goals of elite sections within the national liberation movement and the privileged party cadres deployed to manage the muddled e-cow-nomics system. The reality, however, did not quite work out as cleanly because the ANC's imagined nation's destiny was sabotaged by Zuptanomics, characterised by patronage, cronyism and factionalism (Johnston 2014: 175–180). To be 'resisting transformation' is to a degree to be resisting e-cow-nomics, rather than a more coherent and inclusive national post-apartheid project.

Perhaps a positive closure to this analysis might be found in the following statement about transformation penned by a dean of humanities at the University of Johannesburg (UJ), which appears to encapsulate the new paradigm I have proposed:

> All great universities are multicultural: this isn't a uniquely South African or UJ thing. For me, transformation is not only about fairness for its own sake, nor about redress for previous disadvantage. For me, transformation is about increasing the talent pool and achieving meritocracy: finding the Einsteins in Soweto. The trick to effective

transformation policies is to put measures in place
that will counter biases while enhancing – rather than
undermining – a fundamentally meritocratic, outward-
looking, and goal-oriented ethos. I emphasise merit rather
than fairness because I believe that South Africa will do
itself no favours if it focuses only on the local past; it needs
to look to the global future. I think that transformation is
part of that, since I think it is about unlocking latent talent
in the population.[5]

How does one unlock talent? Semiotics has an answer.

NUTS AND SEMIOTICS

Semiotics – which bills itself as a 'method of methods' – was the
organising theme of a research colloquium organised by the Faculty
of Commerce, Administration and Law, at the University of Zululand
(UZ) in 2013. Titled 'Restructuring for Relevance', it was held at a
local forest lodge. My task was to semiotise the deliberations. I talked
about how meaning is made, what money signifies (sign, myth,
symbol/ideology) and how some departments teach accounting as
a means of explaining how social, economic and political power is
managed. 'Money makes the world go round' sings Liza Minelli in
the film *Cabaret*, but its *meaning* is often lost on student accountants,
we learned. If the humanities study meaning and the bean counters
tabulate the loot, why not mix the two to create a critical discipline
of semiotic accounting studies? A rigorous e-cow-nomics approach
would research how money comes to mean, to make meaning and
to be interpreted discursively. A R100 note, in semiotic terms, 'stands
for' something else (value, status, happiness, greed, power, exchange,
and so on).

    With straight-faced, dry humour, UZ's dean, Nan van den Bergh,
applied semiotics and legal pragmatics as a way of facilitating a

common vision, from the perspectives of the different disciplines. He presented this conundrum:

In the Nuts (Unground) (Other than Groundnuts) Order the expression nuts shall have reference to such nuts other than groundnuts, as would, but for this Amending Order, not qualify as nuts (Unground) (Other than Groundnuts) by reason if their being nuts (Unground). (Her Majesty's Stationary Office, 1956, published in *Daily Telegraph*, 3 April)

Van den Berg's analysis of the above incomprehensible legalese regarding what appeared to be British legislation on 'Unground Nuts' (but not groundnuts, peanuts, tree nuts, coconuts or male 'nuts') parallels the meaningless jargon and logical inconsistencies generated by corporate-speak that substitutes aims and objectives with output indicators.

The nutty professor concluded that the legalese under analysis was a hoax, authored by an anonymous journalist. This is how myths emerge. Myths, which take on the appearance of truth, are utterances without utterers. They exist in and of themselves, irrespective of what is. It took a mischievous study to arrive at this conclusion. The myth of 'white monopoly capitalism' (WMC) was similarly constructed, by the initially shadowy public relations firm, Bell Pottinger. As an utterance without an utterer, it was then popularised by the discourses spread by Zuptanomics and JuJuism, and academically legitimised via the mobilisation of Fanonesque discourse. WMC thus took on the status of 'truth' for these 'aloota' constituencies.

One speaker did examine the lack of 'deep learning' among accountancy students, whose opportunistic aim is to simply pass the requisite exam (surface learning). The discourse of 'line manager' in the academic environment is a surface learning reductionism of deep

learning practices, as should be engaged in by all students and staff.
Here's Brenden Gray's take on the issue of hierarchiology:

> At present, instructions are strategically cascaded from
> executive management via the performance management
> system and accountability measured through various
> reporting mechanisms. Performance targets, KPAs [key
> performance areas] and KPIs [key performance indicators]
> with related initiatives are imposed upon academic
> staff with little or no consultation and are prescriptive,
> controlling and reductive to such a high degree that I
> believe the academic freedom and autonomy of many
> academics at the institution is under threat. Individuals
> are responsibilised to perform when there are in fact a
> number of enabling and dis-enabling factors bearing on
> what is achievable and not achievable over even if what
> we deem as achievable is in fact unproblematic in itself.
> (Gray 2016)

However, the academics do not get to measure the performance of
managers and the executive who are supposed to support this sector.

**Comments on Performance Management (PM) by Brenden Gray
who was head of Graphic Design, University of Johannesburg
(8 November 2012, edited extract from letter submitted to
University of Johannesburg)**

- PM measures an individual lecturer's teaching against
  certain predetermined *quantitative criteria*: throughput
  and average only. It thus has no way of assessing
  the *quality* of a lecturer's performance or it assumes
  wrongly that quantity may be equated with quality.

- PM assumes that the 'output' of the student, or their performance i.e. 'results', is *directly equivalent* to the 'input' of the lecturer. In other words, it assumes that the lecturer is fully in control of their students' learning and productivity (their motivations, circumstances, backgrounds, personal issues, varying levels of aptitude, cultural capital, their willingness, attitudes, ethics and so on) when in fact they are not in control of these things.

- Given that PM both rewards lecturers for good performance and penalises them for poor performance, lecturers may seek to protect themselves ... from the system by manipulating how the students' 'output' is measured and produced; by lowering curriculum standards, offering cognitively substandard assessment opportunities, assessing below the bar and, most worryingly, resorting to authoritarian and transmission style teaching methods to guarantee 'better results' so that they can excel in their performance appraisal ... lecturers may abuse the fact that they are curriculum designers, lecturers and assessors (a conflict of roles) to protect themselves from a measurement system that rewards and penalises them for factors that are out of their direct control ...

- ... the PM system may reward lecturers for unethical behaviour, mediocre teaching, rote learning, the lowering of standards (which ensures good results on paper) and 'punish' lecturers who promote deep learning ...

- ... The student evaluations ... are not evaluations at all but are, in fact, a form of subjective client feedback that can only be used to ascertain that the most basic functions of a lecturer are being fulfilled (timeous assessments, promptness, availability, etc.) and provide no substantial insight into the quality of teaching because students are not experts in pedagogy and may not be experts in their own learning. In effect, using client feedback as a form of teaching evaluation positions the student as a client and thus a passive consumer of knowledge (rather than as a responsible producer) ...

- The system fails to entertain the qualitative and holistic nature of learning, assuming that the responsibility of learning and the quality of learning lies solely with the individual lecturer when indeed learning takes place in complex contexts and situations where the performance of the individual student is contingent on a variety of interrelated factors, some of which are in control of the lecturer and many that are not. The system effectively reduces teaching to a simple input-output model, which is not efficacious in understanding the complexities of teaching, equating learning with social control.

As the head of research at the Reserve Bank Dr Rashad Cassim put it at the UZ conference, coalesce in the tearoom, create teams, talk to each other, go for blue sky and curiosity-driven research, but also offer policy research. Make your work relevant and challenge government orthodoxy. Economists, said Cassim, have largely lost the art of popular writing as they now play with complex models (as now do universities also). It is largely left to Nobel laureates to talk in accessible language with ordinary people. Absorptive capacity is an issue – reports and studies are not read because policymakers are unable to read (because of a lack of time, education, application or stamina). We need to escape the obscure terminology of unground nuts legalese and communicate our work much more effectively to the general populace.

If the Reserve Bank can show such good tearoom sense, why not universities?

Notes

1. Read more at: http://www.teachthought.com/pedagogy/literacy/what-close-reading-actually-means/
2. Read more at: http://www.nihss.ac.za/content/document/consensus-study-future-humanities-south-africa-status-prospects-and-strategies
3. *Strategic Marketing* 2 (2012): 57
4. On first arriving at what was then Natal University I obtained copies of inaugural lectures, among which was one by Tony Voss, Professor of English. His argument problematised the idea of academics working at their leisure in developing intellectual capacity. This value ceased along with the Berlin Wall in 1989, which resulted in neoliberal managerialism running rampant. And it is indicative that the institution no longer has a copy of this subversive text that was published by its own press.
5. Alexander Broadbent, 25 July 2015, internal UJ memo. See also http://youtube/u0S6_IJPAmY

5 *Of Bulls and Bears*

For universities there is no bottom line as they are public services that must deliver employable graduates to the marketplace. The unemployable graduates or evicted incomplete professional students who assume that universities are social welfare facilities go into government and state-owned enterprise (SOE) management where they earn much higher salaries, benefit from huge perks and do less work, without much accountability. Where else in the world would self-respecting graduates willingly associate themselves with bankrupt SOEs, operating literally in the dark ages like Eskom, South African Airways, the South African Broadcasting Corporation, the Passenger Rail Agency of South Africa and Telkom? They might offer good benefits but they offer shoddy service, high prices and attract government bail-outs and never-ending mirth from their critics. Career pathing in such organisations is actually political pathing and the Final Placement Syndrome: it is about the money, cows and patronage. It is not about changing the institution for the better, service delivery or national sustainability.

In contrast, most academics, I think, do take their jobs seriously.

MANAGERS AND FORMS

Some people think that academics teach. Research, as previously mentioned, is what we do after hours when we are not 'working'. What lecturers really do is fill in forms. Forms for this, forms for that: iEnabler, HEMIS (Higher Education Management System), RIG (Research Information Gateway), IRMA (Integrated Research Management Application), KPAs (key performance areas), DHET (Department of Higher Education and Training), OROSS (Online

Research Output Submission System), ORACLE, a multi-model database management system, and so on. Not only do we live virtually in acronym-obsessed software, we also have to manoeuvre through a spreadsheet economy managed by remote upper management. My colleague John Collier's response was:

> I am in no position to make sense of loads of spreadsheets and data lists. Academics are not versed in the specific discourses required to intervene intelligently in this matter, and I have no intention of learning this new lingo ... let those who are trained to speak it, talk the talk. I have long used up the minor percentage of my time that is meant to be allocated to administration. The rest, now, needs to be spent on teaching and research.

Our students, sensing our frustrations and wanting to alleviate theirs, conceal themselves behind doors and bushes, and pounce the moment a hapless lecturer is sighted. A female professor in an understaffed programme when trying to get to the toilet and back to her desk was mobbed by hordes of students when she exited her office, all clamouring for immediate attention as she struggled to get across the corridor. Not to be outwitted, the female students followed her into the toilet while the rest surrounded her on her return. Just going for a pee takes a real act of will when on campus – especially during registration periods. This kind of student pack behaviour occurs when a sympathetic face and an administratively well-informed lecturer can be apprehended.

Students cannot make sense of forms, staff are often bewildered and academics resent being dragged away at peak marking periods to undergo 'training' on how to populate computerised software written by programmers who think that academia is a milk-processing factory. A professor from America once commented in exasperation at his experience in South Africa: 'I've never before worked in a university that has such a lien on one's time.' An instructive comment this, as this was before the mergers, before corporatisation, but after massification, and before all the performance management (PM) and other endless and unstable software was introduced. He went back to the United States for respite – the same country that has instrumentalised the world.

For management, Parkinson's Laws apply, as work means going to meetings and generating more work for academics that needs to be done at night and weekends after the meetings are over. For academics, work requires that meetings be paced with other academic activities. When one is in a meeting one cannot be found, when one is lecturing, one is always found.

THESES, SUPERVISORS AND PUBLIC INVESTMENT

Life as an academic was much tougher (and much more fun) in the 1960s and 1970s. Research funds during the 1960s and 1970s were scarce, as were postgraduate students. Some lecturers were more scarce, usually consulting or playing tennis, but a few did do research. High student attrition rates were encouraged and the statistically significant thirty-three and one-third exclusion was thought to be a fair reflection at first-year level in some departments. Teaching was a haphazard affair.

A bad lecturer lost students while a good lecturer never could find a classroom big enough to house the transfer. In this respect, I must pay homage to Barry Ronge, who regrettably wrote his last column in the *Sunday Times Magazine* in early 2014. Barry-the-columnist was very coy about his career as an English lecturer at Wits in the 1970s. He was the rock star of the department. There was no room big enough to house the crushing throngs of students clamouring for entrance to his tutorials. He was entertaining, profound and engaging. Nowadays, lecturers are surprised if just half the class is in class, and even more so when that half the class that is in the class is paying attention.

Mostly, they just want out, not in, as with Barry. Students now cheer when lectures are cancelled (they are neither audiences nor readers). Barry held us spellbound; he made reading a pleasure and listening to his dazzling lectures was a weekly treat not to be missed. We were always in his classroom. Every column he wrote for the paper was like a mini-tutorial. Now, that's called entertainment education. In those days – the 1960s and 1970s – students actually came to class and a few professors still wore gowns. Hot pants (worn by females) then became the rage. The gowns, suits and ties disappeared as the ageing professors retired. The hot pants remained.

The 1980s changed conditions as universities invested much more heavily in teaching and support. So, when contemporary students claim that the thesis is 'all their own work', I ask them to consider the multiple investments in their thesis made by taxpayers, the university, administrators, committees, supervisors, examiners, mentors, peers, classmates, funders, deans, academic co-ordinators, lecturers, faculty and school boards, senate and other support staff and mechanisms too numerous to list here.

If it takes, on average, 10 000 hours to complete a PhD, diligent supervision could total a notional 1 000 hours. This figure does not include co-supervisor time, seminars and reading groups. Fastidious supervisors put in time, shape the thesis's structure, provide significant intellectual resources and some closely copy-edit and even sometimes assist in writing aspects of the work.

Accepting donor and taxpayer funding places obligations on recipients. Among these are: (i) completion; (ii) sharing of data and information with other researchers on a team project; and (iii) acknowledging sources of assistance and funding. Subject communities also want acknowledgement and benefit. Students who privatise their research do not always apply these principles. A dissertation or thesis is the student's work and is issued in the student's name, but it has resulted from a collaborative process involving many people. National infrastructures underpin every thesis student and at the research universities dedicated offices do so at institutional level.

Think of the complexity: assessment and processing of applications and registration, letters of recommendation, funding support letters, grant application templates and quarterly supervisor reports. Discussion of topics, approval of proposal drafts, presentation of proposals to school colloquia, allocation of proposal discussants, often from external institutions at their own cost, writing up of reports on presentations, submission of revised proposals to supervisors, and then submission to the school's Higher Degree Committees (HDCs). Then from there to ethical clearance committees and final approval by college and university research offices. All this occurs before the actual thesis even starts.

Add, where available, the financial support from universities and especially supervisors when they invest their own research funds into student research projects and sponsor their conference participation. Sadly, the candidate in the published article that results from the thesis often forgets diligent supervisor acknowledgement.

Behind the scenes administration additionally includes bi-annual reports required by HDCs and funders, all of which consume massive amounts of time and effort on the part of supervisors and schools. More reports, filing of comments, discussion at staff meetings, consultations with candidates, sometimes with their parents and their therapists also occur. In difficult cases, students make no progress, disappear for months on end, have to be tracked down, reminded that they have legal obligations in terms of their registration contracts, and often counselled through dark periods of writer's block, depression and lethargy. No good deed goes unpunished, as one frustrated supervisor (David Coplan) observed:

> The tardy, shit-eating external readers and examiners
> who ask how the supervisor could have let this mess be

submitted, while one had to drag the candidate that far with wild horses. I have a record of having gotten every single one of my supervisees their degrees except those who went awol. So I was always given the 'borderline' cases. For my trouble, I was often scolded and calumniated more than the candidate.

All this falls on the supervisor's shoulders, who is thus harassed by the institution, wanting to know why progress is not occurring. This may require more reports, correspondence and meetings with university managers. All the while the dean is barking at the heads of departments who supervise the supervisors because she herself is being barked at by institutional auditors who are themselves subject to national policy on throughput, subsidy and timely graduation – whether or not the student is ready, or signed off by the supervisor. Software – IRMA, RIG, ORACLE – has to be populated and time waits for no supervisor.

Blame is apportioned all round – and the student may be blithely unaware of these considerations or the unremitting stress being absorbed by supervisors, committees, academic leaders and deans – all of whom may be coming up short on their own PM key indicators because of these stresses. The consequences of not meeting their 'outputs' is that staff may be denied sabbatical, forego annual pay increases and deprived of superannuation or honorary status on retirement. So to meet their targets, some supervisors will take on topics about which they know nothing and supervise to the lowest common denominator as Brenden Gray explained in his comments on performance management (see Chapter 4), with the inevitable consequences.

As one of my recently graduated respondents observed, in the face of institutional failure,

> the more tenacious students will fight on, work hard independently and graduate. Their indomitable spirit

will sustain them through poverty, academic neglect, incompetent university staff who never know anything about anything and the disappointment that their peers are just as clueless as they are. When they graduate, the supervisor will be there beaming with pride at having successfully duped another naive hopeful and actually getting rewarded for it with a promotion. The now disillusioned student will either run off into an unfulfilling government job or stay in the system and perpetrate the same crimes onto incoming students. I mean why not? They can get away with it. They will perpetuate this dysfunctional cycle of the blind leading the blind.

This case aside, academics are the only class of professional who are systematically punished for doing their jobs against all odds. There are always the exceptions. In the United Kingdom, students might meet with their PhD supervisors just twice – once when they register and then when they hand in their thesis.

When the miracle of submission occurs, after good supervisors have recurrently read, edited and advised on every single sentence and full stop, the student can finally take a break. For the supervisor, no breaks are permitted as s/he might have ten other students at various stages of their degrees still to supervise and the associated forms to fill in.

In due course the examiners will report – all the while anxious and impatient candidates nag away at why the process takes so long. Some examiners could not care less, which is why the supervisor and committee must select with great care and experience appropriate and reliable assessors. Generous examiners cede their intellectual property rights at no cost to students who draw on their reports to make revisions.

Examiner payments are pathetic. As one former dean (Alexander Broadbent) told me: 'I especially think that doctoral supervisors and examiners are academy organisational dogsbodies: under-valued, under-appreciated and poorly paid.' Examining is an act of professional commitment and love of academia on their part, not always appreciated by those students who squander the time, effort and extreme dedication put into the process by these highly educated slaves-who-are-examiners. While most candidates will knuckle under and do the corrections, thereby improving the work, some opportunistically scream 'foul', threaten legal action and a few opportunists do take the university to court – a South African pastime – in which case they are no longer students but litigants. While things sometimes do go wrong, usually they go right if everyone is doing their jobs in this highly inter-reticulated web of complex relations.

BALLS AND AWARDS

The following definitions of soccer and rugby tell us much about the academic malaise. Soccer consumes 80 minutes, involving 22 players pretending to be in serious pain, rolling about in the field in abject misery. Except, of course, when one of them scores. Then the entire team engages in a writhing group grope worthy of a porn movie. Thirty rugby players, in contrast, spend the 80 minutes pretending *not* to be in pain and might high five or crash into each other when scoring a try. The old adage that soccer is played by gentlemen watched by hooligans and that rugby is played by hooligans watched by gentlemen no longer applies.

Whether in pain or not, the players of both sports at top level earn obscene salaries, though rugby players are also hedging for their future health and potential disability – whether temporary or permanent. They are finished by their early thirties, whereas the soccer group gropers can continue groping for a while yet.

Academics, in contrast, have no sell-by date except as determined by pension funds, institutional retirement policies and the stresses of untenable staff-student ratios, underprepared students and administrative meltdown. Far too many take early retirement just to get their heads back into normal shape and far too many others are put to pasture because they have committed the crime of reaching pensionable age.

The solution: we should think of ourselves as golfers, that rather boring sport where spectators meander across water-sapping greens after (mainly) men who hit little white balls across what one might call a delightfully manicured, peaceful battlefield interspersed with obstacles like bunkers, ponds and the occasional wildlife. All very genteel. Golfers live to a ripe old age still playing. Look at Gary Player. Golfers try to level the playing grounds by means of a mechanism they call handicaps.

However, golfer's winnings, like tennis players, used to be measured in American dollars. Where the rest of us cretins are just happy to bank our meagre monthly pay cheques, top sportsmen and women earn millions. These millions used to be plastered all over the television sports reports along with their scores. Only a few of the golfing professionals achieve this status, making the soccer players look poor, even as they are bought and sold like cows by their clubs in what otherwise might be categorised as legal high-end slave trade.

In the academic world in South Africa, there are the research millionaires who play the right sports (sciences, engineering, medicine) – so to speak – and the rest of us also-rans who play in poor sports (humanities, education). We do not try to hit little white or larger balls here and there, but rather to change the nature of the game itself. We are lucky if we can score but two 'accredited' articles annually, while the big hitters make the Proteas look dismal as they reach hundreds in annual article accomplishment.

This extraordinary achievement – which can only occur through massive funding, the availability of literate and competent lab assistants, a low teaching load, good institutional support and a factory production line – is what separates these superstars from the plodders looking for their balls in the bunker sand. Among the plodders, of course, are those who write for readerships, not balance sheets, indexes or bureaucrats. We thus rarely get out of the bunkers, and when we do, we are reminded that the golfers and the tennis players are the monetary role models.

The monetisation of publishing is my point. Once upon a time when academics made the rules and management followed them, all peer-reviewed journals – whether accredited or not – qualified for internal disbursements of research incentives, if on a differential scale. As with medical aids, the funds earned by the accredited articles cross-subsidised those that did not qualify for this arbitrary qualifying status.

Everyone was happy.

Actually, only the academics were happy. At some point, however, a manager changed the qualifying criteria. The 'unaccredited' journals were removed from the list. As Johan Jacobs, then a research manager observed: 'All other research publications simply became invisible – and with this, a major part of our research in the humanities – and were not included in the annual research publication.'

The University of KwaZulu-Natal at its annual awards ceremonies for the Top 30 researchers has adopted the golfing metaphor. It lists winners of grant applications in rands. The Top 30, however, excludes the top researchers who did not play on the designated 'accredited-onomics' greens, as their courses (the journals in which they published) had not made the DHET lists. These lists work like the Reserve Bank – they set the benchmarks. For example, an invitation to be the external examiner for a PhD from another university was once issued to me. I did not apply to undertake this minimally remunerated, often arduous and certainly thankless task. Confusingly, this university wanted to justify its invitation to me by asking me to vet myself, and for me to categorise my publications into 'accredited' and 'non-accredited'. It was clear that the 'accredited' journals (only those on the DHET list) were to be taken seriously. Since only South African journals can be 'accredited', the *International Bibliography of the Social Sciences* and Web of Science-listed journals not being subject to this classification, it was unclear to me why some busy bureaucrat wanted this division. So I told the university's research officer to take a hike. I don't mind being underpaid to examine but I refused to waste a morning justifying my employment by mindless form-filling.

In response, the department concerned filled in its university's form from my CV. While I understand that examiners need to be vetted, this particular exercise had little bearing on my ability and experience to be an examiner. A bad examiner will be a bad examiner no matter how many DHET-accredited publications they have, whether or not they fill in the forms required by the administrators. We are all embedded in multilayered supporting networks and infrastructures. But these infrastructures sometimes let the academics down, as is illustrated in the next section.

DROPOUT RATES

The Centre for Research on Evaluation, Science and Technology, Stellenbosch University, undertakes surveys of the tertiary education sector. Its director Johan Mouton observed: 'A few universities that have been accepting any doctoral student (no selection/no screening) have a drop-out rate of 90%! Not surprisingly, top universities are imposing more stringent selection criteria at this level.'

One of the corollaries of Murphy's First Law is that 'it is impossible to make anything fool proof because fools are so ingenious' (Martin 1973: 5). Two constituencies are thereby compromised: (i) the fools who apply for PhD studies; and (ii) the fools who admit them. The administrators who set unrealistic 'targets' (for admission) are not themselves responsible for ensuring throughput. That onerous task is cascaded to the hapless, exhausted academic sector that is dumped with the job of doing the impossible, and then punished for failing to achieve their KPAs. The ingenious fools who admitted the ingenious applicants in the first place evade blame. As Murphy's Third Law states, 'Nature always takes sides with the hidden flaw.' Well, now that flaw has been exposed. The fools who admit just anyone to doctoral programmes work in terms of Wozencraft's Law: 'If you make all of your plans on the assumption that a particular thing won't happen, it will' (cited in Martin 1973: 12). A 90 per cent failure rate trumps the 10 per cent success rate. This is also accounted for in Finagle's First Law that states: 'The likelihood of a thing happening is inversely proportional to its desirability' (cited in Martin 1973: 11). The issue here is the inevitability of failure under such conditions and the inevitability of failure of human judgement.

What persuades policymakers and senior management to make such grievous and obvious errors? These start with the way that universities are funded, their need to the pay their bills and the assumption that educational institutions are simply production lines that enrol 'clients' who are processed via the promise of learning on entering a university and pushed out at the other end of the factory a few years later, whether or not they are educated or literate. On graduating students, the university then applies for the state subsidy now owed it, but it rarely calculates the per-item cost of processing the final product/client/student/cow. This occurs because universities are not required to balance their budgets. Rather, they are permitted by e-cow-nomics to endlessly defer their debts – often for ideological reasons. The very costly production line, where 90 per cent of the products disappear prior to final beneficiation, is funded by the hapless taxpayer who is milked to the hilt.

The Wilson Effect is applicable – 'What's good for Lockheed is good for America'. The Lockheed Phenomenon proves two principles: (i) incompetence on a grand scale can be rewarding; and (ii) large bureaucracies (like universities, South African Airways, Eskom, and so on) rarely die – they just borrow more money from the government (cited in Martin 1973: 51). The increasingly dehydrated cows are simply rerouted ad infinitum in a perpetually thinning treadmill.

Some universities accept illiterates because they pay fees or are sponsored by the National Student Financial Aid Scheme (or are trotted out in the name of equity) and thus are exploited as a kind of futures bull market offering vicarious debt security. But the real debt, hidden in the internal accounting, hammers academics and seriously disadvantages the capable 10 per cent of students. As one very capable graduate recounted, the quickest way for supervisors 'to realise their dreams of intellectual super-stardom is to take on more students than they can manage' and 'behind closed office doors, their supervisors drop the facade of care and show them that they are nothing more than performance units'.

Further, the Law of Asymmetrical Supervisory Distribution ensures that the 90 per cent who will inevitably fail will consume 1 000+ per cent of all institutional resources, leaving little left over for the successful 10 per cent – irrespective of whether or not they get adequate supervision. Rudin's Law seems to apply here: 'If there is a wrong way to do something, most people will do it every time' (cited in Martin 1973: 13). As a comprehensive theory of mistakes, this form of delusional accounting appears to assume that it is entirely possible to pick up a piece of excrement by the clean end.

In investigating the 90 per cent failure rate, management demands reports from academics, usually in a highly structured format. The design and issuing of uniform forms becomes uniformly obsessive, setting forth a flood of reports and policy statements, computer runs, new surveillance software, employing ever more technocrats on a treadmill who might know their software (but often they don't). This First Law of Academic Mismanagement punishes the academic sector for problems *not* of their own making. Let's get the operational systems working properly before we change the structures!

Universities employ consultants to reveal the obvious. The obvious, however, is not obvious when it is so obviously obvious. Researchers are able to quantify and reveal the obvious because those to whom a problem should be obvious are obviously academically illiterate. Their optimistic belief in bull markets is counteracted by the pessimistic academic sector's knowledge of bear markets that follow the bull. There has to be a balance. Now, let's talk about the obvious to obviating debt.

SCHUCKSING THE DEBT, SCHUSTERING THE FINANCES

The year 2016 ended with universities attacked by arsonists as the fallism movement paralysed education institutions across the country (Booysen 2016; Habib 2019). This continued into early 2020 until interrupted by the COVID-19 lockdown that included universities being emptied of staff and students, now working digitally.

Anyone familiar with Leon Schuster's candid camera films will know the South African English phrase: 'You have been schucksed.' The #FeesMustFall campaign out-shucksed both the government and university counsels in demanding a '0 per cent fee increase'. Their joint capitulation that killed one of the cows warded off the new revolution just 30 years after the last one had finished. Not bad going for massed bunches of rabble-rousers, some of whom were not averse to burning portable toilets belonging to a black economic empowerment (BEE) firm, throwing rocks at security staff, or burning cars, administration blocks, lecture theatres and science labs across the country. One vice-chancellor caught trying to talk directly to a crowd of protesting students showed that he really could take a punch – just like in the old days when some vice-chancellor were in the thick of things but were then *protected* by students from the Security Police.[1]

'Free education' was in 2016 already costing the taxpayer R41 billion annually. As our embattled minister of education, Blade 'Must Fall' Nzimande, told a disbelieving television interviewer, 'South

Africa has the money. We'll get it from the private sector.' In fact, in our utterly distorted economy, most of the tax is paid by a minority of individuals, the cash cows, who are now paying also for the no-fee option.

The ways in which universities schucksed the debt resulted in the following crisis budgeting mechanisms:

- Unoccupied posts and posts from which current staff retired or resigned were frozen, which means that students get less services for less fees – a fair trade.
- Departments and modules that lacked viable student numbers were terminated, and their staff were redeployed to teach other disciplines. Dead cow lecturers are reassigned to teach in cash cow disciplines, whether or not they know what they are doing. And, we all know what happened in the cadre-deployment e-cow-nomics realm – just look at the SOEs. Their fees never fall and their services never improve – but where are the fallist students in fixing this sorry bunch of losers? As Peter's Spiral explains: 'Incompetence plus incompetence equals incompetence – attempts to relieve incompetence increase the number of incompetents and still there is no improvement in efficiency' (Laurence and Hull 1969: 107).
- Tutoring and graduate assistant posts were terminated – usually senior students who used their income to pay their own expenses.
- Postgraduate funding was shifted to the undergraduate sector and now graduate students were complaining about the lack of financial support for them.
- Universities now commoditise anything and everything. We know about the 'black tax' where an employed member has to support a large extended family of un- and underemployed members. The academic tax includes

parking charges; research funds are top sliced to cover shortfalls; visiting professors may be charged office rent and research grants (many of which employ students) have been slashed. Under COVID-19 conditions, many of us are personally subsidising our universities in our data usage. Academics are now also forced to spend a disproportionate amount of time in raising their own salaries from external sources instead of delivering on their core activities of educating students and doing research.

- Individual academics are now constituted as cost centres and failure to recover cost to company might see his/her termination. But that's okay, because academics are commonly assumed to be underemployed in the first place, though we are the only professional class that works 12+ hours a day for six days a week, paid on the improbable basis of a 40-hour working week and then told to spend 20 minutes accessing and populating computer forms to apply for leave to consult a doctor for 15 minutes. In freeing students from fees, academic staff will most likely become the slaves.

- Universities will corporatise further by enlarging their rentable shopping precincts, replacing Mom and Pop food outlets with branded fast food stores that can pay top rentals. Via this means the cost of food and refreshments will increase in equal proportion to the loss of nutritional value. This will be known as shuck rent.

- The massive institutional costs of re-budgeting and rescheduling, and rebuilding destroyed infrastructure, can be passed onto anyone but the students engaged in this critical pedagogy of deconstruction in this new post-structural accounting environment. The new term is 'huckster shuckster-bookkeeping'.

- One of the students' demands was the expensive insourcing of janitors and security from specialist firms. Well, here's how some American universities deal with janitorism: student assistants polish the office floors and staff clean their own offices. A great learning experience in humility and everydayness. American universities employ their own in-house police forces who pay their way by issuing parking tickets. During COVID-19 the only people working on the University of Johannesburg campus were the security staff and the janitors, the latter with nothing to clean.
- Staff salaries will be reduced, promotions frozen and top performing academics will move to greener, cleaner and more peaceful pastures.
- Toilet paper was saved by shifting from two ply to one ply!

As the University of the Witwatersrand's David Coplan, previously from New York, comments:

> Where I come from these measures are standard procedure and implemented without irony or apology when budgets are cut. I've been through all these and worse in NY, where they were considered uncontroversial. One of my colleagues said to me self-righteously that she supported the students because they paid her salary. So you'd like them to stop paying it? I asked. Needless to say the irony was lost on her too. Nice to know I've not yet been Schustered.

Now we all know why Schuster is our most classless, ethnicless, raceless, but most financially successful transgender and provocative film-maker. In shuckstering us, he creates an imagined space where problems can be resolved by taking the mickey out of everyone – including himself. But even his currency diminished during 2020 when his films were accused of being racist, a consequence of the global popularisation of Black Lives Matter discourse. The Shuckster himself fell when Showmax and DSTV removed his movies from their programming. But no one accused these black economic empowerment (BEE)-owned television stations of screening them in the first place. The managers evaded censure and the director and his producer of colour get the blame as discourses change. What's comedy today is deemed racist tomorrow. Such texts should be studied for what they reveal about audience preferences, satire, conflict and multiculturism as in Schuster and Role Switching 101.

Here's another example of shuckstering as it affects post-doctoral students who are expected to earn their keep by producing articles in accredited journals that earn universities state subsidy.

ALLERGIES AND PERFORMANCE UNITS

When my wheat allergy was first diagnosed in 2000 I ordered a wheat-free meal from South African Airways. This resulted in a telephonic conversation that went something like this:

> Airchefs: 'So, you're allergic to wheat?'
> 'Yes, wheat, pasta, wheat flour, pastry, biscuits, bread, etc.'
> Airchefs: Silence … 'Okay, but can you eat chicken?'
> 'Yes, even if the chicken has been eating wheat.'
> Airchefs: 'Okay, I see. Does this mean that you can eat fish also?'

This bizarre exchange reminds me of some dealings with some research officers:

> Research officer to new post-doctoral student: 'So, you've been here for six months?'
> Student: 'Yes, but for the first three months I wasn't paid. My supervisor had to support me and getting "captured"

on the system and settled in was a nightmare. The first three
months were wasted because of bureaucratic inefficiency.'
Research officer: 'So, have you got any publications yet?'
Student: 'Well, it takes a while to publish in a peer-reviewed
journal, even when one is getting paid and not having to
chase the bureaucracy and begging one's supervisor and
parents for food, rent and transport money.'
Research officer: 'Is that a no?'
Student: 'Yes. Yes, it's a no.'

This kind of dissonant discussion typifies the experience of post-doctoral students everywhere. The Airchefs nutritionist who called me had no idea about allergens and the hypothetical research officer thinks post-doctoral students are all self-financing magazine journalists with monthly deadlines who can churn out peer-reviewed articles in a short time even as the employer fails to administer them efficiently.

The sciences can churn articles out. But in the humanities, being the 'soul of the university', as we're constantly reminded, a two-pager reporting on some lab procedure is not part of the genre. Being the 'soul' takes a lot of reading, writing, thinking, researching and debate. Articles can take 1 to 30 years to germinate, while others can possibly be done in a few months. One wag, Bertus van Rooy, from an upcountry outfit observed:

> I recently raised a few questions about what I perceive as
> the questionable ethics of particularly natural scientists in
> multiple authorships where some authors in all probability
> never read the manuscript, nor the multiple misusing of
> post-graduate students in publishing 'with them' where
> they do all the work. I also raised the point that the farcical
> emphasis on 'recent literature', which serves the purpose
> of basically lifting the 'impact factor' of a journal. It was
> heartening that you made the exact same points.

The refereeing process in the humanities can take up to twelve months. The three to five hour copy-tasting turnaround (rejection) by *Nature* or *Science* is for the humanities an impossibility. If and when accepted, often after extensive revisions, the article is then slotted by the publisher into a production schedule that can take another year or three.

'So, have you got a publication yet?'

Research officers, human resource divisions, insatiable deans and other bureaucrats are never satisfied. More, more, faster, 'Are you published yet?' This is accredit-onomics. Which reminds me of Tom Lehrer's ditty on smut, the voyeur never being satisfied.[2] Reading takes time, it gets in the way of writing; it ruins our performance outputs. (But reading improves our teaching, our knowledge and our research. Reading is the critical cut.) The result of treadmill entropy is more and more hogwash, a recycling mill, products rather than knowledge.

'Are you published yet?'

The writing and publication – which transgresses any idea of 'financial', 'academic' or 'tax' year – is the quickest part of doing research. So, what we are doing – like rats in a maze – is publishing by rote rather than thinking and making a difference. My suggestion is that we institute a compulsory programme for research administrators in which we explain the meaning of the 'intellectual year'. This kind of year, involving slow scholarship, cannot be managed like a factory manages its annualised output. A former British working-class lad whom I met at a semiotics conference in Germany in 2000 told me that he really did not want, like the rest of his family, to work in a soulless factory, with its mind-numbing production lines and designated toilet breaks. So Paul Cobley got himself educated and then appointed at a university; 'Just in time,' he observed forlornly, 'when the university had itself become a factory.'

When post-doctoral students who have just arrived and taken on challenges of getting settled are asked 'Are you published yet', I think of my exchange with the Airchefs nutritionist. We're not speaking the same language – even if it is English.

EDUCATION AND COMMODIFICATION

The #FeesMustFall movement demanded free education, even though the taxpayer already covered two-thirds. In any society, no matter what the economic system, someone is paying or society will go belly up.

Let's look further at who pays when some don't pay:

- Academics will spend more and more time trying to raise funds at the expense of educating their students, doing research or administration.
- Disciplines will be further commodified into the cash cows and the dead cows. Dead cow disciplines like philosophy that are the *raison d'être* of the academy will atrophy and be buried. The symbolic cost will be incalculable.
- The cash cows are massified beyond classroom sizes or the ability of the academy to deliver 'decent education', which means that graduates won't be able to secure 'decent work' in a decent dairy.
- Hugely oversubscribed departments are the first to lose lecturers because they are deemed to be cash cows already paying their way, now assisted by surplus lecturers from dead cow disciplines.
- When students trash their campuses the cost of repair has to be factored into the next year's budget – everybody pays, including the taxpayer.
- Having brought the institution to the brink of financial crisis, whole systems break down, illness rates go up and delivery fails, graduates are tarnished with an associated

negative institutional media image and the institution loses credibility.

There is no such thing as a free lunch. But when the lunch is terminated – as done by Vice-Chancellor Nana Poku at the University of KwaZulu-Natal during early 2020 – the freeloaders respond violently .

#FeesMustFall needed to respect people and property. Though thousands of campus-based anti-apartheid activists during the 1970s and 1980s were sjambokked, shot at and detained by the police, we never trashed anything. For this earlier generation, street protests were a form of public communication, not destruction. Neither did we physically threaten anyone or cause them to commit suicide, as tragically occurred with one University of Cape Town medical professor in August 2018. Bongani Mayosi's 'soul had been vandalised' by rampaging students, his family charged.[3] During apartheid, we kept our classes going. We articulated our ideals and secured the support of the wider community – both within and beyond the university. We did, however, threaten a system and by developing alliances across social sectors, apartheid fell. Intimidating someone is easy. Replacing a system takes time and intelligence and requires popular support across all constituencies.

Lest I be accused of being consistently sceptical, let me balance the equation with some positive comments on deans.

AN ODE TO DEANS OF OLD

Cornuelle's Law – 'Authority tends to assign jobs to those least able to do them' – is here evaluated with regard to some deans with whom I have worked (and mentioned in this book). As an undergraduate student at the University of the Witwatersrand in the late 1960s, my memory of deans is that they were the imperious who sat on high during registration. Their signatures were necessary, so students deferred, were signed in and never saw the dean again. Except, me being the perennial disturbance in the lives of Authority, I did get to engage with them often.

My earliest memory was when I applied late for geography honours. I had foolishly neglected – as students do – to submit my application on time. I was told no dice, no acceptance, go away, by a dean's secretary, a true-to-stereotype Abominable No Woman. So I consulted my departmental head. He wrote me a supporting letter, made some calls, but still no dice. I then consulted the Students Representative Council (SRC) president, Adam Klein. In those days SRCs actually worked for, and represented, students, rather than for political parties and themselves. He listened, then reached for his tie in the draw of his desk, and strode purposively across the courtyard to the vice-chancellor's office. A day later the dean reluctantly signed me on.

Some years later, as a junior academic in film, I cheesed off my new head of department. He had queried the cultural politics I had brought to my new epistemologically rabble-rousing journal, *Critical Arts* and had cancelled my promotion. My previous geography head of department was now a deputy vice-chancellor, so I banged on his door and again requested his intervention. Soon I was in the new Willingman dean's office. A wonderfully likeable chap, not on-high at all. This urbane literature professor told me that heads of departments cannot interfere with committee processes and that my head of department would be educated in this regard. I got my promotion and was then immediately head-hunted to Rhodes University.

Before going to the interview at Rhodes, I was called in by the deputy vice-chancellor. He told me that a hundred phone calls had been received from Rhodes as there was great consternation about my application. The journalism department there was known to be a cauldron of Marxism, destablisation and hippydom. The post had been vacated by Guy Berger who had been imprisoned for seven years for his anti-apartheid activities. Was I going to follow in his footsteps? Guy was not a hippy, dope smoker or a rabble-rouser. The deputy vice-chancellor told me to expect particular questions, and if they did not surface during the interview, I was to pose them myself and answer them.

'Oh,' he continued, 'there's one more thing. The new Rhodes vice-chancellor is the same fellow who as dean at Wits tried to exclude you from geography honours. He'll be chairing the selection committee.' Keith Beavon then roared with laughter and sent me on my way. Well, I was appointed, even though seen to be a Marxist, but not a hippy. On arrival, English professor Nick Visser told me that one of my tasks was to help the other five Marxists at Rhodes restore the integrity of historical materialism as a rigorous analytical method and to disarticulate it from hippy discourses and sloppy personal behaviour with which it had become associated.

Where at Wits I had never been to faculty meetings, which were reserved for the select few, the lower PoW ranks, at Rhodes these were held on Saturday mornings. Efficiently chaired by the dean, everyone consulted their handbooks, and three hours later, a mass exodus to holiday cottages at Kenton-on-Sea occurred. On arriving at Natal in early 1985, I found a very different culture. Faculty meetings could run for two days. No one consulted the faculty handbook. Everything was up for discussion. So democratic was Natal that actual decisions were hard come by. Whereas Rhodes meetings were rules and outcomes based, Natal's were debating chambers with no quarter given – but usually polite, if dogged and robust.

At Rhodes and Natal I learned that deans represented academics and not just Authority, as they do now. After the year 2000, academics were hung out to dry in the so-called transformation process, an inevitable consequence of the mega-institution.

So I partly disagree with Cornuelle's Law in this instance. My experience of most of the deans under whom I served during the days when universities were democratically managed was a highly positive one. But once non-negotiables came down from on very high, deans became administrators and flak catchers with limited discretion or flexibility. Where deans once fought with the academics in the trenches – though some still do – now the trenches are filled with exhausted academics who have no real policy influence on the academy's legislatures.

Imhoff's Law applies: 'The organisation of any bureaucracy is very much like a septic tank. The big chunks rise to the top.'[4] That's a real indictment of any organisation.

BEYOND PATH DEPENDENCIES

Many festering issues resurfaced during 2016. Sections of a big chunk Jacob Zuma's own constituency turned on him after the Constitutional Court ruling on Nkandla. Veteran anti-apartheid newspaper commentator Allister Sparks fell into hot water for suggesting that Hendrik Verwoerd was 'smart'.[5] F.W. de Klerk was pilloried for venerating Boer War generals as resistance fighters against British aggression during the Anglo-Boer War (1899–1902). Afrikaans singer and actor Steve Hofmeyr had punted General De la Rey in particular. All the while 'fallism' was sweeping the country, with Nzimande, Zuma, some vice-chancellors, fees and monuments, but not yet Schuster, being swept up in the movement's path. Fallism as a strategy, however, was monological, lacked a solution, let alone a dialectical analysis. Democratic parliaments are based on dialogical reasoning: thesis – antithesis – synthesis. That's why parliaments have official oppositions. They provide alternative ideas that can be debated across the spectrum. The public is supposed to be the beneficiary.

Elements of the mining industry colluded with the state, unions and corporate greed to wreck this sector – an example being the massacre of 34 miners at Marikana. Poorly written and anti-constitutional government white papers were being spewed out by a random generator machine, especially in the media sphere, exhausting and extending civil society's capacity to respond intelligently to them. SOEs were collapsing, costing and constantly being bailed out by the increasingly frazzled and indebted taxpayer. South Africa's growing international debt secured it junk status from the ratings agencies.

So, why this self-induced e-cow-nomics deterioration? The problem was not with the economy, but with a lack of leadership. We have leaders aplenty. However, when thieving political cronies are put in charge of whole sectors, multibillion rand enterprises, and huge SOEs, can we be surprised that bankruptcy and operational failure become the norm? SOEs that were once efficient, profitable and service-oriented were now wrecking the economy. Delivery relies on good leadership at all levels.

The solution is to break with path dependency. We have entrapped ourselves in the past, trading on victimology, wanting to apportion blame, breaking, burning and looting things that do work. We had become our own worst enemies. Jan-Jan Joubert (2019) fixes the ANC's truly non-racial woefully short period to 1985 to 2001, observing that the party now is busier fighting for a better past than for a better future, that it lacks political will and too often reverts to the politics of distraction. Christopher Merrett underlines the point:

> Redistribution is no substitute for long-term economic growth, which Eskom is unable to support. State-owned enterprises cannot continue to be sites of plunder. Expropriation without compensation will undermine investor confidence. States do not create development or jobs, but rather an environment for enterprise. Race-based entitlement and tender secrecy banish initiative. These are all well-rehearsed in endless lists of national ills.[6]

In contrast, the proverbial lion will find a future-oriented route. Nelson Mandela was one such perceptive lion, Robert Sobukwe and Steve Biko too. As Daniel Defoe's Law on leadership states: 'It is better to have a lion at the head of an army of sheep than a sheep at the head of an army of lions' (Martin 1973: 110). The Constitutional Court, however, suggested that Parliament was dominated by sheep at every level.

Brilliant role models are aplenty. Flawed, sure; racist, sometimes; blind to advice, often. But they show leadership when required. Exemplary leaders come to mind: Thuli Madonsela, Kgalema Motlanthe, Barbara Hogan, Ella Gandhi, Richard Maponya, Desmond Tutu, Vincent Maphai, Joe Slovo, Raymond Sutter, not to mention the younger lions, Julius Malema and Mmusi Maimane and Lindiwe Mazibuko, among so many others. And then of course is the leadership offered by the Constitutional Court and Chief Justice Mogoeng Mogoeng, the sheep who turned out to be a lion.

The media are quick to label brutal dictators as 'strong men'. In fact, they are weak men who cannot rule without violence, as they are unable to earn respect, govern through consent or lead by example. The real strong men and women are those who stand up to corruption and brutality; they take on its perpetrators, no matter what the cost is to them personally. In South Africa, our leaders' VIP protection units outspend by far the tertiary education budget. That's pretty telling about the lack of leadership, the lack of vision and the lack of public confidence in the PoW who currently occupy leadership positions.

In effecting critical cuts, leaders:

- put institutions first, not last;
- represent their constituencies through hard gritty work, they don't ignore them, repress them or exploit them;
- lead by example, don't expect freebies, handouts and entitlement;
- don't expect to get rich, but to rather enrich the practices

of a critical citizenry through enabling humanistic social values and opportunities;

- encourage the social dialectic, consider alternatives, debate syntheses and consult to find the best solutions;
- have integrity; they cannot be bought, bullied or broken;
- have vision; they can see the consequences of a decision before the rest of us can even see the problems on the horizon;
- take long-term views and resist short-term expediency. Mandela and his comrades spent up to 27 years on Robben Island studying and awaiting the moment of opportunity. Then they seized it with alacrity;
- give respect and they earn respect. They don't 'command' respect;
- surround themselves with better leaders; they ensure smooth succession and stability;
- are not narcissistic, not self-absorbed, not selfish or lusting after sycophancy, but have integrity, vision and presence; and
- facilitate discussion, consensus and outcomes that serve the greater good.

EXTERNALING AND SURVIVING

African universities in the British Commonwealth take exams very seriously. Woe betide students (other than in South Africa) who can't spell or write grammatical English or who write messily. Exams are assessed as much on form as they are on content. Content aside, the actual practice of examining is little more than a medieval bartering arrangement – 'I'll external for you, if you'll external for me.' How else will we persuade each other to do this drudge work? In addition, we squander our diminishing leave allotment when we have to go to other campuses to examine.

The paperwork required of the cows to get paid by some institutions is hardly worth the fodder. The endless forms sometimes require duplicated information and furthermore want certified documents of bank accounts, identity documents, proof of residence, tax status, wife's/partner's identity documents and marriage certificate, details of dependents and proof of life.

All South African forms impertinently inquire as to my 'race'. DNA testing aside, there is no official definition of who is what – other than, as during apartheid, how we look to the bureaucrats. My African-American colleagues and Africans in the diasporas tell me that I share with them 'the black mind', yet in South Africa I am told that I am 'white' (see Tomaselli 2018). The rest of Africa doesn't care. Philosopher John Collier's email tag stated: 'All brains are the same colour.' I refuse to play the game even if only for 'statistical purposes', a politically correct euphemism that ignores the grey matter common to all of us.

International examiners are often flown to where the African campuses are located. On entering the hotel room, one is dwarfed with scripts stacked from floor to ceiling, the assessment of which consumes a week of utter torture in badly lit and seriously uncomfortable surroundings, often being buzzed by malaria-carrying mosquitoes. I won't even discuss the appalling food at the dodgier hotels, though when at a Swazi Southern Sun, the chefs know when underpaid academics have arrived, as they tend to spirit both lunch and supper in vast quantities from the breakfast room since only the first meal is included in their booking.

One year the University of Swaziland distributed its many examiners across a number of hotels. To my relief, I was allocated to the Mountain Inn, a delightful garden venue with good food and a good view. At the end of the week we were all rounded up and taken to the bank to get paid in cash, where we compared accommodations and argued with bank officials whose recurring annual stock e-cow-nomics response was that they didn't have sufficient reserves to pay anyone. But always, after some phone calls to the examination officer, the cash miraculously materialised, though in Ethiopia the Reserve Bank to which I was taken once claimed that its vault was empty, could I please return the following day? Having later secured the local currency, one then had to locate the black market to convert it to dollars, since the birr was unconvertable.

A group in Swaziland had been once put up at the Happy Valley Motel, where the eating place was across the parking lot from the rooms. Outside the rooms prostitutes hovered, day and night, pouncing on the male examiners whenever they exited. That hotel was subsequently taken off the list of approved establishments. In Zambia, with law professor David McQuoid-Mason, we once shared university residential quarters with some members of the Zambian soccer team who got up to all kinds of high jinks more suitable for a Happy Valley kind of venue. In Maseno and Eldoret in Kenya, I was placed in once grand hotels well past their primes, though after a few bottles of Tusker beer, things looked and smelled better. The Sunset Hotel on Lake Victoria had to carry hot water for my baths up eight flights of stairs and had, in those pre-cell phone days, but one working telephone in the manager's office.

Once engaged in the daunting task of external examining in these countries, I began to actually enjoy the work, though for much of the time one is on autopilot as one wades through thousands of scripts. By being taken to the scripts, rather than the scripts being sent to examiners, examiners are isolated from endless distractions caused by deans, auditors, students, family, student protests, burning tyres and tear-gassed offices, and resultant campus closures back in South Africa. It's a liminal and peaceful existence requiring that the job be done in the time allocated.

In contrasting this African experience with my PhD examining for European universities, and their externaling for us, one realises the stark differences between Europe and Africa. Whereas African universities encourage in-depth, almost scopic, research, overseas universities prefer lucid brevity. Northern examiners often complain about the length of theses from Africa, even though they are paid in dollars, whereas the locals just get the local skimmed milk.

The European oral – what they call a 'defence' – is basically ritualistic. Once, when I had just got into my stride, in came a trumpeter wearing a medieval costume blowing his ancient horn. I was cut off mid-sentence and everyone was vigorously marched out of the venue to drinks. Sometimes the defences can become a battle of wits, but the student will have been passed already, irrespective of the critique unanswered at the oral presentation. The thesis, published as a book – whether corrected or not – is in some cases already printed for distribution at the ritualised defence.

However, in Europe the PhD student is treated as a person – despite flaws in the assessment process. In South Africa the student is present only in the text/thesis and the examiners are initially unknown to the author. It's a socially alienating process conducted by administrators and couriers (now the Internet). In Europe, students sometimes get to choose their examiners, whereas in South Africa the process is usually anonymised under a cloud of confidentiality for fear of legal action.

We need to rise more to the occasion here. The African emphasis on form (spelling, grammar, structure) would go well with the South African emphasis on argument, wrapped up in a more humanistic European-style ritual.

What happens when errors are not corrected? The next section offers some killer examples.

HAZARD AND SAFETY

One of the laws that was derived by one of my students, Arnold Shepperson, who started his degree at the age of 36 in 1985, after working as an electrician on the mines, goes something like this: 'The likelihood of a disaster occurring increases in proportion to the educational level of management.' In other words, disaster is likely to strike when the professionally certificated managers refuse to listen to the workers on safety (and academic) issues.

The Tongaat Mall labourers knew that building codes were being violated in late 2013 when the structure collapsed. The contractor had taken short cuts and removed scaffolding before the concrete had set. The owners, who lacked building permission, were 'sorry' for the death and injuries caused. They assured the council that the contractor had guaranteed safety but, as the press soon revealed, the mall developer had his dirty fingers in many municipal and other tills.

Shepperson's Law had been warning mine management in the early 1980s that a switching gear on a mineshaft was faulty. He was ignored, belittled and told to mind his own business; that he was not a qualified engineer and didn't even have a diploma. Eventually, the inevitable happened and eight miners died. That the union lost the court case – despite his testimony – further eroded Shepperson's confidence in the value of education. So he decided to enter the belly of the beast – the educational institution – to find out what dementia ails it.

In registering for electrical engineering, his worst fears were soon realised. The curriculum, he said, was idealised and in his view did not address the kinds of daily problems that workers faced both above and underground. So he shifted to English and Philosophy. Perhaps via these disciplines he might be able to make sense of how certified professionals make nonsense of sense and why they can't see the wood for the trees. But sometimes they can: the engineers' warning about a seal flaw went unheeded. Consequently, in 1986 the *Challenger* space shuttle was launched against their advice – only to explode 73 second later, killing all astronauts on board.

In Philosophy Shepperson bumped up against logical positivism. In English he learned about how literature shaped the Anglo-Saxon world view of culture, problem solving and how the world is interpreted. Neither explained his lived experiences on the mines. So he registered for Cultural Studies in his search for a theory to explain the misuse of power, hazard and safety and of how to develop strategies to deal with these issues (Shepperson 2008). In the case of the mall, it was the power of the owners and the contractor to ignore the law, to pull on political networks and to discount hazard.

With the mine incident, Shepperson, who was already reading Immanuel Kant's (1998) *Critique of Pure Reason* at the coalface, was ignored because his reading habits identified him as 'learnéd'. All he had was on-site experience, clearly muddled by also reading also Heidegger and Wittgenstein. Like with the Tongaat Mall construction labourers, the (ill-educated) but certified supervisors and managers dismissed him as a crank. Knowledge is not power in these circumstances. It is a burden because the workers know that the managers are putting their lives in danger.

Shepperson's research delved into historical discussions of culture, literature and applied semiotics to make sense of how the mining industry and the legal system made sense of hazard. How does culture and ideology blind one to the real material world where concrete slabs collapse, lifts crash, runaway trucks cause massacres and space shuttles explode?

Why is what is so obvious to uneducated and uncertified victims of hazard so opaque to better educated supervisors, managers and owners? The workers in these instances were are not blinded by power, ideology and output imperatives but by the culture of fear – fear for their safety, fear for their jobs and fear of loss of self-esteem. The owners responsible for mining and construction disasters fear little, as their lawyers will protect them. In the political realm they have tame doctors in tow who will diagnose them as terminal and being freed from jail, when they will resume their former golfing ways. Just ask Shabir Shaik and former gangster-police commissioner Jackie Selebi.

But few in Authority listen (Chisholm's Third Law). Environmentalists, for example, have long known that 75 per cent of emerging infections are zoonotic in origin, accounting for billions of illnesses and millions of deaths. These scientists have repeatedly warned about impending pandemics emanating from animal trafficking and Asian wet markets (Wittemyer 2020). But even now few are listening. We are too busy looking for bargain deals and protecting our turf.

TERRITORIALITY, TEACHING AND TEA ROOMS

Remember that film and television series *9 to 5*, where a bunch of gorgeous secretaries never seem to do any work, gossiping all day? When I first arrived at Natal University in 1985, mornings-only secretaries would take two-hour tea breaks. Fridays were trading days at Wits in the mid-1970s as cut-price, pre-packed bags of delivered groceries substituted for spaza shops. Every department had its hawker, usually of senior rank. Everybody was shopping for a good deal and little work got done.

Corporatisation and spreadsheet management changed all that. Few departments still have time to take tea once or twice a day, or keeping up the appearance of academic collegiality. If every tearoom was turned into an office or seminar room the space problem would disappear. Tearooms are protected by departments as was East Germany by the Berlin Wall. Even in the United States where the idea of a tea break is unheard of, a colleague commented:

> I wondered what kind of world it would be if all departments, centers, schools, and such were evaporated. I think the same would happen here as there: the folks with the entrenched Tea Rooms (we have a kind of equivalent – those departments who maintain a 'Department Meeting Room' versus those of us who use a classroom between classes) would still meet with their ilk and hash out 'issues' of importance to them. (Andrew Causey, personal communication, 1 September 2015)

The Territorial Imperative, penned by pop sociobiologist Robert Ardrey (1966), came to mind when I read a headline of King Goodwill Zwelithini opportunistically lodging a land claim for the whole of the KwaZulu-Natal province, while also demanding reparations from the British for the destruction of Ondine in 1879. The second thought I had was the idea of the 'imagined nation'.

Indeed, everything in the social sphere is imaginary, including the fact that the original inhabitants of southern Africa, the so-called Bushmen, are popularly thought to have been nomads, with no fixed abodes. In fact, they always had systems of clan rights to specific water holes and regularly traversed the same routes. They did understand the idea of 'property' as they moved between pans, even if Jamie Uys's *The Gods Must Be Crazy* (1980) pseudo-ethnography suggests otherwise. Still, many later-by-far in-migrants who followed the Bushmen are demanding 'return' of 'their' land while the always-frugal ≠Khomani submitted just one claim in the Northern Cape to where they were pushed by colonisers from the north, south and east.

The Territorial Imperative describes the evolutionarily determined instinct among humans toward territoriality and the implications of this behaviour in human meta-phenomena such as property ownership and nation building. Ardrey's First Law 'is a law of nature that territorial animals – whether individual or social – live in eternal hostility with their territorial neighbors' (cited in Martin 1973: 53).

Just as kings and queens imagine what their empires have been, or might have been, so do academic departments. The rigid territoriality that exists within institutions is remarkable. One of the mandates with which I have been entrusted by my various employers has been to breach territoriality, to facilitate inter-faculty cooperation. While some manned the disciplinary barricades, many of my Centre's allies contributed modules in transgressing territoriality and in re-imagining theory. For a few years (1985–1994) we were successful in breaching departmental boundaries at the University of KwaZulu-Natal and flouting Ardrey's Law and in re-imagining the academic enterprise. We even had tea together. Then the South African Qualification Authority (SAQA) came along in the mid-1990s and returned us to our disciplinary silos marked by our physical territorial haunts.

Much of Brenda Gourley's tenure as University of KwaZulu-Natal's principal during the 1990s was characterised by her attempts to dismantle the idea of disciplines (conceptual territories) linked to departments (physical territories and the basic unit of administration). The motivation behind this move was cost efficiency, right-sizing and all those neoliberal critical cuts that were then sweeping through the global economy. The final institutional victory occurred in 2004 when schools absorbed what previously were departments and colleges absorbed what were once faculties and the big chunks rose to the apex of the new management pyramid. Disciplines did not disappear because they were still linked to occupied territory (offices), the manning of the ramparts (security gates) and the same old departmental signs remained because a depleted budget could not afford to replace them. Heads were recast as co-ordinators without authority or budgets and, mysteriously, overnight those departmental secretaries who survived the purge, were now centralised as school administrators. Not knowing what to call themselves anymore, 'disciplines' reappeared without departments. But disciplines still stopped at the front door of entrances and exits.

In the face of the anti-disciplinary and anti-department onslaught, how did disciplines retain their distinctiveness? The answer: tearooms. The dominant departments had always had tearooms, while the rest of us, cramped for space, just had kettles. The well-appointed tearoom disciplines rarely invited staff from the kettle disciplines for a cuppa. When we did drop in for a chat, we felt like intruders. So we sullenly drank our tea in our offices while we worked and lost out on regular socialising and collegial refreshment.

Students have never got their heads around the idea of schools and they still call the disciplines within them 'departments'. They need something concrete with which to identify, as do staff, who still imagine their tearooms to be disciplinarily bounded. Discipline equals nation and nation must be protected. But this is a false incubation as it is based on boundedness. At my current school at UJ, when three spatially intermingled departments separated from two into three adjacent but separate corridors; the first spat between them was over continued access by staff from each department to the coffee machine in the common reception area. Fortunately, we were all reminded by an alert dean that we are all in this together.

Departments, schools and faculties are merely 'administrative conveniences', as economic historian Bill Freund always reminded us in meetings. These conveniences merely operate at different interacting levels.

Rebuilding collegiality will best start in a common tearoom. It's the smallest building block in the pursuit of the new social transformation. Remember, in the United States in 1773 a revolution started with the Boston Tea Party. Tea is powerful stuff, especially when it is bobbing about in the harbour and reappears as a political constituency 150 years later.

When will institutions re-imagine themselves as a collegiate, sharing and civil society that shares its tearooms?

Notes

1. Read more and see the video at: http://www.politicsweb.co.za/politics/ max-price-punched-by-fallist-protesters--uct

2. See video at: https://www.youtube.com/watch?v=iaHDBL7dVgs

3. *Sunday Times*, 5 August 2018

4. See more at: http://www.barrypopik.com/index.php/new_york_city/ entry/the_organization_of_any_bureaucracy_is_very_much_like_a_septic_ tank_imhoffs

5. Read more at: https://www.biznews.com/sarenewal/2015/05/12/my-verwoerd-comment-wasnt-smart-sparks-tries-to-put-out-critical-fire

6. https://www.fromthethornveld.co.za/will-south-africa-be-okay-17-key-questions/

6 Publication, Rankings and Abacus Management

I first came across the term 'bean counter' when visiting the New York School of Cinema Studies in 1982. A well-known film professor was regaling all and sundry at the entrance to his world-renowned programme about the damage being inflicted on education by bean counters (academic auditors). I had no idea then what he was talking about. However, as narrated in the previous chapters, 30 years later, South Africa had caught up with this neoliberal practice, passing off this commodification as 'transformation'.

Many South African universities have – for better or worse – linked individual research grants to publication in journals accredited by the Department of Higher Education and Training (DHET). The state pays universities a nominal incentive of R120 000 for each article published in particular lists. Opportunistic rent-seeking behaviour is one of the results, but a positive has been the massive increase in publication output, some of it seminal in nature. Clinging to the coat tails of the incentive have come the opportunists, the predatory journals' publishers (Mouton and Valentine 2017). The provocative heading assigned to Jonathan Jansen's (2020) complaint with regard to this rent-seeking behaviour was 'Racket Science'.

In 1982 South African Post-Secondary Education (SAPSE) was merely a blink in an Afrikaner nationalist educational auditor's eye. Implemented within the decade, it continues to rule the economy of research at all universities. Calling it the DHET does not change its spots. 'Is your journal accredited?' is a recurring question I get as editor of two DHET-listed international serial publications. The query reveals that the enquirer is employed at a South African university.

This query will soon be followed with, 'Can my article be published in your *next* issue?' Usually, our next issue with available space is two years hence. Bewilderment follows. 'But I *need* the publication incentive. I've got conferences to go to, auditors' reports to complete, promotional applications to make. Your journal is my ticket to the moolah. Why are you putting obstacles in my way?' Thus are editors treated by their own colleagues as mere pro bono service providers, pay clerks, rather than as academic enablers and innovators. The publish or perish syndrome has aided the corruption of genuine scholarship.

Undesirable publishing practices have been debated at Academy of Science of South Africa (ASSAf) meetings with journal editors and the opportunistic milk-seeking (rent-seeking) perpetrators have been identified. But whether they have been disciplined by their own universities is unknown. The problem is that the emphasis by universities is on quantity and not quality, as quantity brings in the cash that pays institutional bills. Incredibly, some universities permit their authors to take home a portion of the incentive as taxable income. The incentive is meant to build institutional research capacity, not personal bank balances of the fully employed. That is where the problem lies, as internal university policies are in some cases very lax and open to misuse and abuse. This is not the case at all universities and most academics have used the publication incentive funds for the public good, to fund and employ their students, to build capacity, to cover research expenses and to retain the services of retired and underemployed professors who do legitimately bank some of their DHET incentives.

While there are many benefits to both the institutions and individual researchers in publishing in accredited journals, the two recurring questions are indicative of publication for the sole sake of securing funds, rather than publication (also) for the express purpose of targeting (local and international) readerships and having an impact in the discipline. As John Collier observed:

I was told long ago that one per year publication was
very good for a philosopher, with a two-year lead time on
average. In Logic it is much less. Some areas in biology,
like systematics, can yield ten or more a year, if you choose
the right sort of taxa. However, we seem to have a one size
fits all philosophy. David Kaplan (logician with about one
paper every three years) and Paul Grice – philosopher of
language (seven papers in his whole career) – would be
failures here, despite being top of their respective fields.
I sold my soul to the devil this year to get R=4. It was
surprisingly easy, but I could have been making more
useful contributions to my field that might have been
published in non-SAPSE venues. Abacus management
breeds mediocrity.

DHET is aimed at encouraging the *process* of research and publication,
the financing of research capacity and the building of a research
environment. The basis of its derivation was to encourage scholars
to take research seriously in the 1980s, though ideological undertones
were always present.

The misuse of the publication incentive has fashioned a new
intellectual apartheid, one that does not recognise journals not
on the DHET-qualifying lists. Submitted books are audited, if not
read by DHET assessors, as they come back from Pretoria with
staples puncturing the covers, colour highlights running through
the Contents pages and stickers marking specific chapters. This
mutilation of books, sometimes priced at thousands, is indicative of
the bureaucratic rather than the inquisitive mind. The DHET counts
only numbers of publications and ignores the impact of publication
on respective disciplines. Given the nature of the exercise, it can do
little else. But the funding mechanism opens the door to snake oil
comparisons.

RANKINGS AND LINEARITY

I was recently pondering cricket rankings – much as one does publication and university rankings. It is all in the statistics – but meaningless. Here is a cricket analogy: DHET makes no distinction between a bowler knocking off the specialist batting top order and the red ball fodder at the end of the innings. The difference between a Dale Steyn and the rest is who he gets out.

This profound insight I came to one weekend when surfing Google Scholar, as one does when one is bored over a hot and humid Durban weekend when one gets temporary relief from prying academic bean counters. So I did some quick-thumb statistics of my own. In the humanities, books are much more prestigious than journal publication. No one asks about your last journal article, but our colleagues perk up when a recently published book is mentioned.

Different organisations issue different rankings, calculated differently and read differently. The number-1 research university may, in the broader scheme of things, be number 400 if a different measurement system is used. Measurements are often meaningless because it is not clear what is being measured or how.

The supposedly impartial nature of rankings is based on what Chris Brink (2018) calls their 'relentless linearity' and their negative impact on society. Linearity, Brink argues, assesses outcomes that collapse multiple dimensions into a singular continuum. Such arbitrary measures of excellence privilege the few and create cultures of managerial control: 'Rankings and league tables, quality as a positional good, meritocracy as rank order of worth, society stratified into classes, hierarchy instead of diversity ... are all linear representations [which] compress reality into a rank list in which higher up means better and lower down means worse' (Brink 2018: 227). Linearity as the singular way to measure excellence, he argues, betrays the soul of the university. In the top-ranked universities, undergraduate students may never interact with a tenured professor, but the opposite may be commonplace in a bottom-ranked outfit. For the former institution, Waffle's Law applies: 'A professor's enthusiasm for teaching the introductory course varies inversely with the likelihood of himself having to teach it' (Martin 1973: 103).

The realisation that the bean counters are homogenising output and restricting progress came home to me as I was writing an obituary for my recently departed colleague, Stuart Hall. Hall's seminal work in cultural and media studies, literature, sociology and politics, among other disciplines, changed the way that the humanities globally now goes about its business. Hall rarely published in journals and when he did, it was mainly in the form of debates, rather than clearly delineated, stand-alone, incentivised, credit-earning 'research outputs'. He never earned a PhD, but every book and chapter that he wrote had more impact than a thousand PhDs and all DHET journals combined. His many and influential co-edited anthologies would be considered by DHET to be but non-qualifying textbooks. Such works are simply not counted, even if they are highly cited.

Then I looked up other germinal scholars like French philosophers Michel Foucault and Manuel Castells whose work is cited ceaselessly by humanities students and researchers across the world. All the citations are to their books, not their articles, if indeed they generated any. So what does this tell us about accreditation myopia? These august folks might not be considered top researchers by our universities. South African research can be thereby partly likened to the Galapagos Islands, where Charles Darwin developed his theory of evolution. These islands offered the perfect laboratory because of their remoteness, species and geographical isolation. I fear that for all its intended merits that DHET (in the humanities at least) is encouraging much South African research towards evolutionary stasis.

In this context, a Stuart Hall would battle to get funding, a Foucault would never have left the starting block and C.S. Peirce, the greatest nineteenth-century American philosopher, would never have spawned the global industry now mining his unpublished work well over a hundred of years after his death. Psychoanalyst Jacques Lacan and linguist Ferdinand de Saussure, whose unpublished work was compiled by their students after their respective deaths, would be nobodies and Einstein, well, who is he? Just a patent office clerk. Mary and Louis Leakey spent over 50 years excavating in East Africa before they found the fossil that changed world history; time and significance that cannot be measured. Nobel Laureate Peter Higgs of the 'God particle' says he had become a bean-counting embarrassment at his university.

Neoliberal audit mentality collides with field practicalities, research procedures and the very idea of indigenous knowledge systems (IKS). One of our number discovered on his return from a remote rocky outcrop at which we had been doing archaeological research that his museum's vehicle had been fitted with a tracking system. His boss observed that the vehicle was stationary in a single location for most of each day during the week that we were on site. To measure productivity and return on investment, the implication seemed to be, the vehicle should MOVE! Constantly. Next time we will employ a driver to move the vehicle back and forth as a cover for those who want to get on with real stationary work.

Now, I wonder how the Leakeys would have explained that they had spent 24 years working largely in a single valley, Olduvai Gorge in Kenya, before they found a fossil. How does one publish about finding nothing? Then, how does one write about a single find, a jaw? Not only would they have been fired, their vehicle would have been impounded and the origins of humankind might never have been discovered. In fact, the English astrophysicist Arthur Eddington, who proved Einstein's theory that space and time bends, did so in the field, on a West African island, by taking photographs of stars during a solar eclipse. But *he* was NOT moving, so maybe he forfeited his salary? Yet, it was Eddington who proved that space and time are relative. He and Einstein got the plaudits – no thanks to the audits.

Audit culture might have discouraged Darwin from visiting the Galapagos Islands and the corollary that the theory of Intelligent Design would not have been necessary. What if Einstein was told that he was wasting his time doing obscure mathematics, instead of MOVING about, giving the impression of being busy, and feeding vehicle-tracking data to his disbelieving managers? What if Eddington had been denied his funding application to test the theory of relativity from a site on a different continent?

The very discoveries that feed audit culture are those used by the auditors to impede the academic enterprise, the free flow of ideas and even of working in the field. The plaudits are for the audits, not for the raw data or knowledge generation. That humanoid robot, Data of *Star Trek*, has more humanity than those who think that a stationary vehicle in a remote valley is an indication of sloth. Yet, ask those same auditors to check out what is being done way out in the bush: they will reluctantly arrive in their city suits, Gucci shoes, ask for iced water and wonder why their cell phones don't work. What's next? We all get fitted with microchips that report when we're sitting still, contemplating the mysteries of the universe.

Now to my IKS point. The downpours and wind trammelled us by night and the sun toasted us by day. Roads were washed away. At night we desperately clung onto our tents on the edge of the rapidly rising Orange River. During the day we worked with members of the ≠Khomani who shared with us their interpretations of the engravings while they entered GPS co-ordinates. Few think that the descendants of the First People have opinions on such art. Paradigms are more usually fought out between scholars. The gods were speaking to us, insisted the ≠Khomani, via the engravings and the weather and in our interactions.

They despaired at the researchers slaving away under the relentless summer sun when it was better to sit under a shady tree or rock at midday. We explained that research auditors require evidence of output; that the suited People of Worth (PoW) were coming from Pretoria on our last day to check that the site existed and that we were working at it. Our budget and leave requirements would not stretch to extra days on site while we waited for the sun to cool. Here was very sensible indigenous advice, which we all elevate to something special in these postie post-apartheid times. But such advice is depreciated by an instrumentalist system of budgeting that cannot afford it and monitoring mechanisms that cannot accommodate it. Maybe we do need to go back to basics? Why can't we just work when it feels right?

Moving does not equal productivity. Moving, said architect Frank Lloyd Wright is a disease called 'mobilitas' (Baker 2014). Mobilitas, a symptom of academentia, is evident in management as they whizz between campuses, dragging behind them long-suffering academics who would rather work in a single place/classroom/office than appear to be busy by moving all the time. The auditors have shifted expectations to Wright's other term, 'stabilitas'. The expectation is no longer that we produce quality work but that we send fast and dirty articles into DHET-accredited journals.

Forget about the Leakeys with their single-minded lifetime project exposing human origins. Punish Darwin for delaying publication of the *Origin of the Species* (1859) as a result of his fear about the ideological implications of the theory of evolution – which in the current conjuncture places auditors at the apex of the evolutionary pyramid. Discipline the doers, those who get their hands dirty in the field by changing the space-time relations now enabled by vehicle-tracking companies.

All this reminds me of the stereotypical London's bobby's command, 'Now then, move along – don't loiter'. Are we academics not allowed to loiter anymore, doing slow and systematic scholarship while we contemplate the deeper meaning of the cosmos?

The time of groundbreaking academic discovery led, in many cases by unpublished, idiosyncratic and quirky scholars, may be largely over. From here on, it is the bean counters who will rule our daily research lives. Single discoveries that might take a lifetime of research will be punished by the auditors, though welcomed by the Nobel Prize committee. My money's on the latter.

The DHET incentive, creatively managed, remains a wonderful capacity-building initiative. But its instrumentalist application within universities and its opportunistic appropriation by many authors will hasten the demise of fundamental research that actually changes the world. Remember the story about the goose that lays the golden egg?

Why have universities confused achievement with income? Bertus van Rooy, North West University's director of the UPSET (Understanding and Processing Language in Complex Settings) Research Focus Area, wrote to me:

> I sit on a number of committees at the NRF [National Research Foundation], usually language-related, but sometimes also as a more general representative of humanities and social sciences, and it is striking to see how different the profiles of the social sciences and humanities researchers look from the natural sciences. The more highly rated researchers often have h-factors on the ISI/Scopus that exceed 20 or 25, whereas top humanities scholars are sometimes not even found in such indexes, because they write (in) books. My alternative argument to the managers is to look at the ratings, that gives at least some indication. It is not a perfect system, but clearly, if someone is a B, with a relatively low h-factor, his/her peers surely appreciate the substance of their contribution more than someone with C and an h-factor of 15 or whatever.

Increasingly, academics are wading through this kind of jargon, h-factors, impact factors, download indices, citation matrices and all those acronyms and associated spreadsheets that like uncontrolled viruses have taken over our academic lives and lingo in the vain pursuit of public accountability, market positioning and productivity. Good scholarship is under stress as we tread the production conveyer belt at the same time as trying to cope with injuriously elevated enrolment targets, unanticipated staff and tutor cuts kick in, modules are cancelled and staff-student ratios reduce the possibility of our offering good education, let alone 'good scholarship'.

Certification-driven students (and their parents) appear to be quite happy with this state of affairs. These students gravitate towards easy options, in some cases their lecturers are complicit in this flight from excellence, as they seek the lowest common denominator. Everybody except the 'good scholars' are happy. The intellectual illiterates are then accepted into graduate studies and we all hope for the best despite the ominous signs of academic meltdown – this is the Finagle factor at work.

One counter-practice is offered in *The Para-Academic Handbook: A Toolkit for Making-Learning-Creating-Acting* (Wardrop, Withers and Rolfe 2014). Para-academics critically reflect on how the idea of a university as a site for knowledge production, discussion and learning has become distorted by neoliberal market forces. Gary Rolfe (2014: 1) coined the term 'paraversity', a subversive, virtual community of dissensus that exists alongside and in parallel to the corporate university.

The critical cuts enabled by 'para-academics' operate across and against the corporate agenda of what Bill Readings (1997) calls the 'ruined university'. The ruin's mission is the generation and sale of information (the so-called research agenda) and the exchange of student fees for degree certificates (the teaching agenda). In South Africa, this is paradoxically legitimised by the term 'transformation'.

Para-academics create alternative, open access, learning-thinking-making-acting spaces. They don't worry about career paths. They take the prefix 'para-' to illustrate how they work alongside, beside, next to and rub up against the all too proper location of the Academy. They make the work of higher education a little more irregular, a little more perverse, a little more improper. Para-academics just continue to do what they have always done: write, research, learn, think and facilitate that process for others.

Para-academics do not need to churn out endless 'outputs'. They work towards ideas rather than quantifiable 'products'. The only problem with para-academics, as one post-doctoral fellow remarked, 'is that there is no job security and often they slip into the fractures of a neoliberal capitalist university model that does not offer tenure'. Thus these para-academics live a very tenuous existence; they are the jobbing precariat, the new class who have no expectation of permanent employment or the benefits associated with it. Their zeal is such that they are sometimes accused of wanting to be poor on purpose.

PURVEYORS AND PERMISSIONS

'It's amazing what you can accomplish if you do not care who gets the credit,' said Harry Truman, the 33rd president of the United States.[1] I read this in *The Mercury* on the same day that I filled in my NRF rating report. The NRF wanted form fillers to quantify 'Own contribution', as, for example:

- Conceptualised idea for research;
- Responsible for data collection/analysis/design;
- Lead author writing up of article;
- Wrote first draft, editorial input;
- Postgraduate supervisor of the lead author;
- Owner/co-owner of intellectual property of research;

- Co-developed and executed research;
- Project leader/budget owner.

Imagine all those busy bees at the NRF trying to come up with anti-para-academic categories like these that disaggregate which ideas, sentences and paragraphs different authors may have conceptualised, written and of which they claim individual ownership. This kind of commodification has even reached the outskirts of the known world. 'My words have value,' a semi-literate informant in the deepest of the deep Kalahari Desert once told us. Two rand a word he wanted when talking to us. This fellow would approve the NRF's attempt to tie us grant recipients up in knots. For the indigenous, at best, researchers are a nuisance, but they are also a welcome income source. For researchers, bureaucrats are a nuisance. The NRF not only wanted this information for 2012, but for every co-authored article that rated researchers had published!

To assist the NRF I propose a software programme that will sense the authorial fingerprint of sentences, link these to their utterers/writers and then send the data fragments to a mainframe read through a permissions spreadsheet. From there it will be approved for NRF input and keep all those bean counters busy, who spend their time trying to peg ratios of academic labour, how they collaborate and audit who owns which fragments of the final published outcome.

One global publisher (let's call it P-Way Ltd.) requires of each author the following to be entered into a spreadsheet:

1. Assess whether permission is required.
2. Collect all the information required about the material to be used.
3. Enter the instances where permission is required on the electronic spreadsheet by using one spreadsheet per chapter.
4. Write the relevant permission number on the documentation.

5. The electronic spreadsheet and the hard copies of the documentation mentioned above need to reach the publishers with the final manuscript.

This is proof positive that idiotic instrumentalism is not confined to research or educational institutions.

Here are some of the comments from P-Way authors who were contributing to my volume, *Making Sense of Research* (2019), later published by a local press without these requirements:

> In my chapter on postgrad students using search-engines like Google for their research papers I make partial use of users' online comments. How do I get permission from users called 'Anonymous', 'UsainBolt', 'The Olympics Suck', 'JoyStick' or 'Batman-is-Vladimir-Putin? (Nyasha Mboti)
>
> From whom I would ask for 'permission' for Government Gazettes, Parliamentary Hansards and the SABC Annual Reports? All these documents are in the public domain, and are quoted from in newspapers, business reports, etc. It is ludicrous to imagine that I need to get permission from the Government Printers for these items. (Ruth Teer-Tomaselli)

My own response to the publisher was that these conditions would destroy every academic convention by which we are required to conduct our research and writing practices. Where some sources, authors and publishers cannot be found, are dead, out of business, lost in the mists of antiquity, or unknown, permissions will not be forthcoming. Ethnography as we know it will cease; oral history will die and primary research will be done without reference to any research that has preceded it. If these conditions continue to be requirements, academics, para- or otherwise, will drown in paper, permissions and Pearinda (a medication for high blood pressure).

Most fundamentally, if such a permissions regime is imposed, the very dialectic by which academics construct their arguments will fail, as no one in their right mind will want to cite, paraphrase or cross-reference, as the very act of citation will require the above time-consuming and exhausting P-Way tasks. The convention of embedding current research in acknowledged prior published research will cease entirely. We will spend more time trying to track 'ownership' (allocating who gets the credit to the nth decimal point) than actually being productive. And, the stock currency by which academic work is peer-acknowledged – citation rates and impact factors – will be thus also shattered. Thompson-Reuters and Scopus would go out of business.

While I understand that the bean counters need to separate the passengers from the workers, the P-Way way is inappropriate. Copyright, permissions and royalties are key to the publishing industry, but to turn academics into purveyors of permissions is extreme. For every academic writing, there will be fifteen bureaucrats counting.

Like Monsanto's genetically engineered, non-germinating seeds, every aspect of academia, every sentence written, every new idea, will become copyrighted, trademarked and patented, with the Orwellian P-Way police checking on who owns fragments of statements, kernels of ideas, new words and how these can be charged for.

Remember my informant: 'My words have value!' But no one will cite them for fear of infringement and the bill that will follow.

PUBLISHING AND PERISHING

The analogue age was characterised by snake oil salesmen in the United States and became associated with medical fraud. Pyramid/ Ponzi schemes emerged a century later when finance capital became dominant, followed in the 2000s by the banking meltdown as a result of reckless lending and unregulated markets, and of course the narco economies are an enduring blight. The digital age ushered in the 419 scams, trading on individual gullibility. Yes, we all foolishly imagine that we have an unknown rich uncle or aunt somewhere wanting to warehouse his/her millions in our bank accounts.

In tandem with the above, threats to the academic sector are growing daily, what with predatory open-access journal invitations cluttering our mailboxes, and now predatory conference organisers also.[2] These scamsters sport illustrated websites and organise phantom events run by ghosts and conference committees in places like Washington, DC or in Johannesburg. Where predatory journals with fake impact indices but real bank accounts will offer twelve-hour reviewing turnaround and publish even scientific garbage, as has been proven by article stings conducted by *Science* (Bohannon 2013), now there is a new set of threats facing editors of legitimate journals. The current threats include cloning, theft of titles, mimicking appearance, stealing websites, articles, and appointing fictitious board members.

Brokers offer to 'place' articles for authors. Others claiming to be guest editors offer complete thematic issues, ready to print, immediately.

Editors of overseas journals remark on how they are sometimes bullied to publish substandard articles by South African authors, often to the astonishment of these submissions' reviewers, whose helpful suggestions are ignored by both authors and editors and the paper published as was first submitted. When I and my colleagues have queried such ill-advised action, the editor's response has been thus: (a) 'we felt sorry for the author, he's from Africa you know' or (b) we were bullied or (c) we needed to fill the space. This kind of paternalism does the academic enterprise no good at all. While these journals are not 'predatory', sometimes their authors are.

Many South African universities now require their master's and PhD students to publish from their theses and some simply require a publication for a master's degree to be conferred. So editors and reviewers are now having to process opportunistic submissions on a scale not previously experienced, without any recompense for the labour, time or administrative costs incurred by publishers, whose voluntary editorial boards are already stretched to the limit. Journals and reviewers are thus made into unwitting accomplices of institutional degree assessment processes. The journals pick up the cost of this duplicity.

'Publish or perish'. This phrase has been around for a long time. Yet, even today, the many who do not publish, do not perish. Their lack of publication productivity units (PUs) may be punished in one way or another, but nothing that the labour court can't handle in their favour.

The digital age, however, sees new threats as scammers across the world, especially in Pakistan, China and India, develop the new 419 phishing model that rips off inexperienced academic authors desperate for publication. South Africans have been largely shielded from these conniving predators, one clear benefit of the DHET journals and book regulation and reward mechanism.

'Predatory publishers' are creatures of the Web, lurking in the dark deep electronic ditches, prowling through conference programmes and appropriating email addresses from university websites. They prey on academics, students, anyone who needs immediate 'refereed' publication – for appointment, tenure, resource, promotional and PU purposes. These often-unsuspecting individuals are hunted down and sent beguiling, personalised, multicoloured invitations to submit papers to journals with improbable and grammatically incorrect titles – for example, *Journal of Advance Research* or the *International Journal of Science and Technologe*. Naive authors with deep pockets are promised immediate review (within 48 hours), referees can be suggested (Mom and Dad, a neighbour, or pay one recommended by the publisher), publication within the month, while self-plagiarisation is encouraged – submit an already published paper, or take a published article written by someone else and put your name on it. Cutting and pasting from the Web is the new norm. Thousands of these titles are on the prowl.

Predatory journals' websites are replete with grammatical errors, misspellings and appeals to one's venality. The sites, titles and even the layout are often cloned from legitimate journals.

Authors are invited to join unlisted august editorial boards by editors who provide only a first fake name. These phishing exercises work on economies of scale – they list up to 300 open-access titles per publisher, just waiting to ensure that your immediately published article in any discipline will offer the hapless author the next best thing to celebrity status. These mega publishing outlets are run from untraceable Web addresses, fake post office boxes and rundown store fronts. But they do sport real bank accounts. Maybe you are on the board of a journal you do not know about? If so, pay up.

The claim made by these open-access journals is that they will attract readers and citations. The article-processing charges might be waived for authors from poorer countries. Fear not, the publisher will have stolen your copyright and sold it onwards to other desperate authors who think they have been approached by a kindly uncle in the third-hand article business.

But there is more. Your paper will be entered into a lottery draw for a free annual membership of a fake disciplinary association that is managed by the same phishing publishing procurer. Or authors will be invited to phantom conferences scheduled for august places like Oxford. What more could an author want: fame, recognition and disciplinary status? But the conference room will be a chimera.

What is delivered, however, is impaired reputation and embarrassment when one realises that one has been swindled. But again, this can be a bonus where university human resource divisions fail to check out the CVs of applicants who proudly list predatory journals among their academic output. These journals manufacture their own impact factors and one or two even get accepted by key indexes. You can fool some of the people some of the time.

In the pressure to publish, novice authors fail to check these titles, to study back issues or to do any research into the very publications that hold their careers hostage. They become victim of their own carelessness and impatience. To apply the e-cow-nomic metaphor, you have two cows, you clone them, rename them, multiply them and cede your rights – and willingly pay the scammer dairy to steal them.

In China, academics have been encouraged to write in English and to find safety and prestige in Clarivate Analytics that hosts the Web of Science index. In South Africa, the DHET lists play this regulatory role, but the racket science gaps have been exploited by opportunistic authors and universities.

SELFIES AND PUBLISHING METRICS

As with selfies (been there, done that!), China's fast trains (300–400 kilometres per hour) are a metaphor for its desire for high-speed inclusion in global academic discussions (getting there). Intercultural communication, business linguistics and English-language competence are top of the national agenda as China 'goes abroad' following its rapid rise to global prominence economically, militarily and diplomatically. Its scholars are making sense of the West by mining and rigorously reading, critiquing, deconstructing and reconstituting the seminal Western philosophers and theorists, from Hegel to Hall. They have been doing this at the same time that Philosophy is now a threatened discipline in the West because it does not pay its way.

But like us in South Africa, Chinese academia has been also entrapped in the limited horizons imposed by mindless publication-o-phobia led by managers who themselves rarely publish. Where we have our own flawed god (DHET), China selected the Social Science Citation Index (SSCI), the Arts & Humanities Citation Index (A&HCI) and WoS (Web of Science, now Clarivate Analytics) as its benchmark for quality publishing. SSCI is an indicator of specific sets of extrinsic inter-journal quality, and not necessarily the intrinsic relevance of particular journals. Both systems are populated with bewildered emergent academics being told to publish in English where feasible, where to publish, but rarely *how* to publish, whether or not their work even merits publication.

Metrics, while indicating immediacy, rarely recognise the latent longevity of intrinsic value such as in the humanities. Metrics cause academics to engage in short-term thinking, rather than longer-term, blue-sky research, from which applicable scientific and social benefit might eventually occur – for example, DNA sequencing, electric cars, vaccination, solar power and so on. It took over a hundred years for semiotics to become a standard cross-disciplinary method, with undergraduate media studies, language, literature and biology, as just some examples.

Some thinking – like research and publishing – takes time, sometimes a lifetime. Instant publishing selfies are harmful. As Dewey, a young Chinese lecturer with whom I work, observed of his experience at conferences involving senior Chinese philosophers at which I presented my cultural studies analyses:

> The majority of the people we met in China during 2015 and 2016 are just like what you depicted. I am not sure if you can imagine that even some respected [academics] approached *me*, just because I seemed to be close to you, editor of a [SSCI, Clarivate Analytics) journal! During such talk, I was picturing how disappointed they must be when they searched my name. I know they would do that because they seek for Clarivate in the Chinese academia another form for power in a full-fledged Confucian way. To do research is not an undertaking for knowledge or understanding. SSCI means higher title, bigger chance to win grants and getting published again, better pay, higher status. If that is the case, how many people can wait to

be successful? Such things are way more important than knowing and discussing. The only thing people care is 'he has xx SSCI-indexed publications' and nothing more. (28 November 2016)

It is no surprise, then, that D.W.L. Everitt, once a dean of engineering, observes: 'The modern flood of publications contributes more to confusion than to understanding in the world' (cited in Martin 1973: 21).

THE PUBLISHING FACTORY

In the old days – 1973 – my honours class at the University of the Witwatersrand was huge – seven in total. A few PhDs and master's students milled about. Some actually finished. The non-performers were eventually ejected from campus. Some lecturers did conduct research and publish, and a few were internationally renowned. They had the time, the motivation and in my department, Geography, students were encouraged to publish. Quality counted. Our lecturers shaped the discipline globally.

One PhD thesis by Keith Beavon actually called into question an entire sector of urban geography by redoing the arithmetic of scores of articles he had been reading for his topic. He found that some seminal work was full of errors. The result was that a dominant international trajectory of urban geography was chucked out of the Wits Central Block's window.

Despite lecturer exhaustion, the push to publish and perishing by stress, has now become so preposterous that journals across the world are suffering from an epidemic of retractions and legal actions. Many articles (and their authors) are no longer trusted as evidence when cited in court cases.

Sceptical, careful, systematic scholars remain the bedrock of the academy. They take nothing for granted, they think about the impacts and consequences of their work and behave ethically. It just takes one failed article or charlatan academic to affect the value of a degree.

Publication was less fraught in the good old analogue days. The rules of thumb were that you:

- submitted articles to the journals to which your university subscribed, which you read and in which your colleagues published;
- considered journals published by, or known, to your disciplinary associations;
- trusted bona fide publishers known to librarians and the scholarly communities to which you belonged; and
- scrutinised editors and editorial boards, and checked if any were known to you, your colleagues, thesis supervisors and so on.

Such journals did not panhandle for submissions, but issued calls for papers where appropriate.

In contrast, the publishers of predatory journals leverage the 'publish or perish' syndrome; they milk the insecurities of emergent, undiscerning and impatient academics and if what is offered sounds too good to be true, it's because it is. Identified by forensic librarian Jeff Beall as 'predatory', on account of their aggressive recruitment of authors, theft of intellectual copyright and lack of peer review, this sector eliminates barriers to learnéd publishing. Characteristics of predatory publishing further include:

- lack of added value: no peer review, no proof reading, libel checks, marketing and promotion, no copyright protection, and no archival back-up;
- hidden publishing fees and surcharges, usually invoiced after submission;
- retractions permitted on further (extortionate) payment; and
- operating like retailers, offering freebees, discounts,

payment plans, bulk buying, use of PayPal to conceal destination of payment.

The counter-arguments *for* predatory journals include claims that they:

- contest Western hemisphere big publisher dominance;
- question the hegemony of peer review and myopic methodologies, such as occurred when Galileo and Copernicus broke with the Church's teachings (Feyerabend 1975: 14–15). And, 'if knowledge production is to include contestation of dominant ideology, it means the principle of "anything goes" should prevail' (Feyerabend 1975: 19);
- provide entry points to emergent scholars supposedly denied by the established journals; and
- accept whatever is submitted and therefore do not engage in 'censorship', racial or gender exclusion, or other discriminatory practices such as peer review. The unacknowledged discrimination is whether or not the author can afford the publishing fees and/or is concerned about copyright theft.

But is this 'science'? What would be the implications of free-for-all publishing? It was in these kinds of below-the-radar 'anything goes' journals in which the AIDS denialists first published their counter-narratives, because legitimate, properly peer-reviewed journals sensibly declined to take them seriously. The consequences of lack of peer review and fast-tracking opportunistic medical claims can be catastrophic, as was the case in South Africa during the early 2000s. This was one reason why the South African government outlawed claims of fake cures and medical disinformation during 2020 with regard to COVID-19.

ASSAf, the NRF and DHET are now acutely alert to the predators and who publishes in them. These organisations rather want academics to make a difference.

PUBLICS AND POPULISM

'Academics can change the world.' However, there is a rider, says Savo Heleta (2016). Academics must stop talking (only) to their peers. Academics are not rewarded for engaging with the public or when publishing in popular magazines, newspapers and other platforms (which might include television, performances, radio, exhibitions and blogs) from which most people get their information. Knowledge is assumed to occur only in a mysterious set of obscure journals known as 'accredited'. Mucking about in the popular media is seen to be frivolous.

This was not always the case. Maintaining town-gown relations was once considered important. If universities are in the business of shaping society, inventing techniques and technologies, and solving conceptual problems, academic activities and knowledge must be popularised. Our funding largely comes from the public and the public must benefit. That is the whole point of *The Conversation*, sponsored by a consortium of universities.[3] Where few academic articles are cited in the academic literature, individual stories on this Web magazine can attract millions of readers. When academics talk only to other academics, they use specialised language, largely incomprehensible to everyone else, isolating themselves within disciplinary discourses. It can take decades to learn to write accessibly.

Fundraising by universities is enhanced when their work is promoted in language that the public and donors understand. My role model for the civically engaged academic is the physicist in the television cop drama *Numbers*. He applies mathematical solutions to predicting criminal behaviour for the FBI. Now, that is research that is useful, has public benefit and can also get written up in calculus and published in peer-reviewed journals. The programme is also education entertainment as it makes maths sexy, exciting and useful.

When we do finally learn how to write accessibly, our own peers sometimes turn on us. Some of my IKS manuscripts and books have drawn scathing reviewer responses. 'Good for the local newspaper' or a travel magazine, was what one wit wrote on my manuscript on cultural tourism. He was really enjoying himself by complaining about my manuscript's easy reading. I know who he is. Discourse analysis, impenetrable as it is, can indeed be useful in identifying those who think they can protect their anonymity. By being 'critical', Eurocentric and denying home-grown theory and methods, my nemesis was able to ignore the innovative critical indigenous methodologies developed by my multi-ethnic, multigendered, multiracial, multilinguistic, multinational, multidisciplinary team in our work among Kalahari communities. The book was published anyway (ironically, in Europe).

Our indigenous hosts are the ones who argue the most for writing that they can understand. They want inclusion, participation and recognition. They want to be part of the academic value chain. Jargon cuts them out. When writing is accessible, the cry is 'Not academic!' This is what we are told by reviewers, but not by publishers, who are held hostage by assessors who use decidedly unacademic language in making their points.

Rather, we must jabber for each other in obscure code (Pinker 2014). Even when I do write obscurely (as may be necessitated in taking on obscurantism as Arnold Shepperson and I did in an article on the (ir-)relevance of post-Freudian, post-Lacanian, and contemporary Žižekian psychoanalysis in the study of African film (Tomaselli and Shepperson 2011), this too, gets the goat of critics who recognise imported theories and critiques only. Then, ironically, I was hammered by a NRF rating referee who complained about my 'difficult writing'! Difficult writing is what normally is rewarded and cited. Western post-theory offers a one-size-fits-all academic grand narrative, nowhere better articulated than by social theorists who ensure that all the usual suspects are cited, swept up in a heady orgy of name-dropping in every other sentence. It is very difficult for those on the theoretical margins (or with different approaches) to be recognised by these incestuous citation cartels.

If our Kalahari sources have taught us anything, it is this: academics work in frameworks that work for them rather than axiomatically also working for their subjects/objects of study. They argue that Afrikaans is an indigenous language and that land reform is based on a misreading of history (in which their ancestors were the first participants). Our approach to IKS is to examine the researcher-researched relationship and to re-articulate it from an observer-observed gaze where the power lies with the academic to draw the line around Them. We want to find out how our hosts draw the line around us. And, then, what is happening in the negotiation.

In journalism, more accessible than scientific writing, the conclusion or findings start the articles – or used to, until newsrooms juniorised. The inverted triangle ensures that the most important information is provided first. The semi-waffle follows, followed by the real waffle, eventually petering out at the end of the story. This enables the subeditor to cut off the copy without compromising its information with regard to column-inch considerations.

Nowadays, subeditors seem to be language graduates who think the inverted triangle is archaic geometry. The result is repetition, redundancy, the story's object getting lost and lack of focus. With some PhDs that I have marked, 500 pages later, one is still searching for the research question.

ETHICS AND DOCUMENT TRASHING

Recently, I had to clear out 40 years of printed field interviews to comply with an ethics directive. Among those documents were thousands of pages of open-ended transcribed interviews we had conducted in the field with our research participants. These interviews were done before the new bio-medical ethical requirements came along in 2013 that required the destruction of data after five years that flushes useful data through the shredder. As if information, like baked beans, has a sell-by date! How would the world look had Aristotle's writings had been trashed? Along with this indigenous knowledge cleansing goes history, memory and the personalities that populated these forms of tracing.

In rereading the interviews, tears came to my eyes, as I scanned transcripts with characters with whom we had worked for nearly twenty years, many of whom have passed away, in communities where the death rate is way higher than the birthrate. The causes are illness, old age, AIDS, substance abuse, malnutrition, domestic violence, the winter cold, and homicide. Whatever the cause, I experienced a sense of real loss in trashing the transcripts. Here were the stories and thoughts of individuals who wanted to be on the academic record, to whom we had returned hard copies of interviews, but who had nowhere to archive them. These same individuals played international roles in movies, human rights movements and in research.

Our Kalahari hosts always welcomed us into their communities and their sense of self-significance was captured in our published work. They worked with all disciplines (geneticists, zoologists, botanists, archaeologists, astronomers, linguists, anthropologists, pharmacists, historians, literary scholars, development and tourism researchers). They redefined the nature of the research encounter: they claimed to be the professors and positioned all these visiting professors as their students – why else would they be consulting them? How many academic careers did they make for visitors like us? And yet, what they told us had to be trashed, for ethical reasons, we are told. Who benefits from this documentary vandalism? Certainly not the folks who talked with us. Nor the organisations that represent them. Nor their children who want to remember them.

Science is not just survey work, then abstracted, sanitised and discussed in terms of statistical significance. In these forms of encoding, personalities are eliminated, feelings discounted and hopes lost as the academic factory processes the human experience into explanations often unrecognisable to those who provide the data, the stories and the information. That is the nature of the academic enterprise, however. But it is often an alienating one for our hosts. They think that we academics have lost the plot somewhere.

In the mid-1980s a group of American museumologists kicked up a stink because they encountered a life-size diorama of 'Bushmen' displayed in the Cape Town South African Museum natural history section. It remained open to the public until 2000 and the traditional ≠Khomani leader, Dawid Kruiper, went to the Museum especially to see the diorama. The diorama was 'archived' in 2001 because the politically correct positon insisted that the life-casts be regarded as human remains and are therefore never to be exhibited. The archaeologist responsible for managing the exhibit facilitated a cleansing ceremony with traditional healers to dispel negative forces. The leaders of various Khoisan groups want their history and culture to be shown in the Iziko South African Museum, which they regard as the most appropriate place for the story of the First People to be told. Here, they will co-habit with exhibits from Egypt, Greece, Rome and the Near and Far East, thus recognising their international influence.

Dawid Kruiper, the traditional leader of a group that came in the 1990s to be known as the ≠Khomani, whose land and heritage was declared by UNESCO as a natural heritage site in 2017, told my team that when he died that he wanted to be part of that diorama in the Museum. Political correctness, however, would not allow his wish. Nevertheless, Dawid's death in 2012 was appropriated by 2 000 opportunistic politicians and dignitaries who used his international prominence to polish their own marbles. They bulldozed a section of the communal, land-claim farm for a huge tent and two car parks, graded the road, installed portable toilets, served themselves a hot meal, made frothy speeches and gave take-aways in polystyrene containers to the Kruiper clan who were told to sit in the sand and sun outside the marquee (Grant 2012). Now, you tell me what's ethical and what is not. I won't again paraphrase the Kantian categorical imperative here.

The shredded transcripts had outlasted many software programmes: Wordstar, Xywrite, ASCII, Wordperfect, Microsoft Word, all lost in translation, often faded in dot matrix print format, vanishing before our eyes. Dawid and his ≠Khomani clan have outlasted the opportunists who sought to abuse his memory for their own ends. Many academics, film-makers, photographers and journalists have worked in partnerships with such communities to help restore dignity and trust, to enable mutual benefit and the establishment of archives. But this work is not easily recognised by the academic enterprise. University publishers continue working within archaic assumptions about what is 'scholarly' and what is not. Higher degree committees impose their own positivist prescriptions. The South African Qualification Authority (SAQA) roots syllabi in fixed moments. Classroom auditors demand banking education rather than critical pedagogy.

Academics are expected to be aloof from real-world concerns, distanced from the effects of poverty and theory- or survey-driven in generating 'findings'. The contemporary lived relations that we study are unsettling for our critics, as indeed they are for us. Academics are conventionally supposed to conceal their feelings, while promoting 'objectivity'. The anxieties that result from making sense of the mess that typifies observer-observed relations are findings that are not admitted.

We can learn from the First People about reversing observer-observed relationships. The next chapter takes closer look at subjects of research looking at us and how they help us to look at ourselves.

Notes

1. See https://www.brainyquote.com/quotes/harry_s_truman_109615
2. See Jeff Beall's 'List of Predatory Publishers', 2016, https://webmail.ukzn.ac.za/
3. See http://theconversation.com/africa, which observes that a well-functioning democracy requires an equally well-informed citizenry

7 Writing Africa and Identity: Shifting (Our)selves

WRITE! oh Africa WRITE!

Write, for it is RIGHT

Let's WRITE for the nations to see

WRITE for them to read, so they'll understand

and then know how we feel

Written is better than spoken

Spoken is easily forgotten

Spoken is better when written

Written can be passed on from generation to

generation from one to another

Written is permanent, never loses meaning or taste.

Let's speak silently, they will hear us so loudly.

Let's fight right and nobody gets hurt when we WRITE

Let's bridge the gap between races, nations and cultures

And display our diversity in language, food and music

WRITE about the pantsula, the traditional dance and ballet

When written it will never be forgotten

Let's WRITE Africa,

For the Nations are patiently waiting to see our great writing.

(Mhlongo, cited in Mbatha 2013: 10)

Mhlongo's poem is used here to inaugurate this chapter as a way of highlighting why curiosity, writing and reading are crucial in studying and doing research. On one field trip to the Kalahari in the mid-2000s graduate students recurrently uttered the word 'random' to refer to anything that grabbed their attention, something that was novel, an odd event that required some kind of colloquial signifier. 'Random' was soon evacuated of any meaning and simply became a marker that marked some empty exclamatory rhetoric that signified 'we're connected'. Field trips generate team work, offer memorable common experiences and the camaraderie that develops clearly distinguishes the exuberant life of departments that do field trips from those that don't. Lifelong bonds develop between students and lecturers,

Though many departments take their students off campus for practical exercises, I was once threatened with disciplinary action because I had dared to vacate the concrete neon-lit, airless classroom that resembled a prison and head into the bush to work with the !Xoo in Botswana, as we had being doing for eight years. My so-called line manager, of a much lower rank, harangued me, telling me that the university offers a 'service' to students that requires that we remain in the classroom at all times, teach out of a book that someone else has written and treat students as 'clients'. This from a self-proclaimed postmodernist. Well, the students told him off. He whimpered back to his swimming pool.

The common utterance 'it's academic' is mischievously meant to indicate that an academic's explanation has no merit. We are said to be living in an ivory tower, a place disconnected from reality. Such critics are correct when myopic line managers try to prevent real-world learning, as occurred in the above example.

I remember one excursion by the second-year Geography class at the University of the Witwatersrand in 1972 to what was then the Eastern Transvaal. Apart from the fact that our lecturers had us running up and down mountains every two hours day and night taking temperature readings, we also were required to map the distribution of anthills on various plains and in valleys. Three groups tramped the area and came to the conclusion that the distribution of anthills was random. One team, however, insisted that it was uniform.

So we laboured through the cold winter night reworking the numbers on manual calculators, which had whirring handles and pinged all the time. Not only did the pinging and click-clacking keep everyone awake, but exclamations of bewilderment rang through the darkness. The original findings were confirmed every time: 3:1 for random. Now, we all know that statistics are only as good as their assumptions. Faulty assumptions result in garbage findings. After many hours of noisy frustration – and wondering just what the one group was measuring – the lecturer consulted a map.

He asked if there were square holes next to the alleged anthills? 'Yes,' answered the errant team.

'You **^% geo-idiots,' he yelled. 'Since when are anthills accompanied by square dugouts next to them? Do you even know what an ant looks like? Those are prospectors' mounds – from the last century!'

Well, imagine using foul calculus like that! Nowadays, someone would take offence and institute a complaint. No one did. We all learned from the experience – we now knew that getting the assumptions wrong means getting no sleep – as well as that history does count. The prospectors must have been laughing in their graves.

Just proves, what do academics really know? At least ants know that they construct their hills randomly and then they watch in amazement as the human number-crunchers get the arithmetic right and their assumptions wrong. I am always fascinated when broadcaster Jeremy Maggs interviews academics. He puts them on the proverbial spot when he starts with: 'Now, what can an *academic* tell us about (insert topic)?' One is already on the back foot, wondering how to justify the academic enterprise. Well, we can count and measure but we can't always read (the landscape).

Applying for leave for such field trips can be bewildering. The leave categories that now regulate the factory floor at the University of KwaZulu-Natal are anachronistic in learning and research environments. Innovation falters, creativity is muted and lateral thought is narrowed. Certainly, the fictional Professor Charlie Epps, a physicist and FBI consultant in the television series *Numbers* could not do either of his jobs (which exist in a synergetic relationship) if he had to negotiate such a byzantine leave system. The fictional FBI would be all the poorer for it. So would physics, maths and crime detection.

From the age of thirteen, my daughter accompanied some of my research teams into the Kalahari, where over a ten-year period she set the place alight research-wise. Researcher-researched encounters change dramatically when teams include unusual members who behave unconventionally (see, for example, Dyll 2003). Publications, thesis chapters and videos resulted, adding to the body of knowledge relating to guest-host relations. Boring factor analysis comes alive, regression analysis moves off the axis and the variables can be manipulated to identify surprising, even scientifically unexplainable, occurrences. These new 'findings' (observations) expose flaws in old certainties and predictable bureaucratic-led categorical ways of doing things. The ways that researchers manage their families while doing research have been discussed by only a few anthropologists.

One question is how to accommodate young parents who want to do field research. How to justify the expense of children travelling and the reorganisation of the working day/night are enough to give any honest auditor a real headache. The spreadsheet economy cannot accommodate such situations and how to ensure that the costs incurred by travelling academics with regard to their children are legitimate may become a contentious issue for auditors.

For longer trips to the Kalahari, students were issued with a fifteen-page survival guide. Among the items mentioned were:

On site, students and staff are expected to stay in research mode while awake. (Dreams can also be important on these kinds of field trips.) All participants must be constantly vigilant in observation, recording, and note taking, in asking questions, and making conceptual connections. Many opportunities for checking data and previously obtained information are lost because researchers don't always use the opportunities available to them. Show initiative; don't just do what you are asked to do by the lecturer. This is not a holiday, nor a jorl.

Depending on numbers of students, whether or not we are staying at a camp site, water is rationed to between 5 and 10 litres per day per person, for drinking, cooking and washing. That's not a lot of water, so most water should be used for drinking and cooking. Food is also rationed. Obtaining further supplies from Ngwatle is very expensive: a three to six hour round trip (depending on the state of the road) over a 4x4 track, and very high prices in Hukuntsi (four times the cost of the same foodstuffs in Durban). (We have had situations where a single individual has selfishly and unadvisedly chomped a week's rations in three or four days. Pace your food consumption, or the research team as a whole will find itself with inadequate supplies.)

Researching the African Ivory Route in May 2018 with my team revealed to me just how transient life is. We survived my 4 × 4 Nissan Patrol sliding over a rock-concealing, mud-slushed, steep gravel road down the side of a mountain just after a storm. One of my tyres was mortally wounded and eventually blew on the highway back to Johannesburg. Fortunately, we had lived to drive through the Fundudzi Sacred Forest and to walk through the largely dried-up lake where the spirits still rule. On a later trip we communed with the mystical white lions at the Global White Lions Protection Trust Reserve, and talked to Linda Tucker and her team about multi-species ethnography and how to save the planet.

But on the last day, following a guide over a very derelict footbridge that lacked handrails at Phiphidi Waterfalls, on stepping on a (rotten) plank, it cracked, and I hit it with my chest very hard as it tilted up and I fell down. Fortunately, I did not fall onto the rocks below or impale myself on half a metre of exposed nails. I have consequently revised the Park's catchphrase, 'Nature at its best, smack into it with your chest'. My shellshocked body was retrieved by Varona Sathiyah just before I was about to fall through, thankfully saving me from prematurely meeting my maker. She and the guide, both in front of me, were just one or two steps ahead of death. The last time I experienced such shock, pain and broken ribs was when an oncoming car crossed the white line in Empire Road and hit me head on when I was eighteen. In those days cars did not crumple and my family ended up in hospital, but the front seats had just been fitted with safety belts, which saved us. And, astonishingly, the offending driver was not injured and could not have cared less about the harm that befell us.

I recovered from the footbridge accident, but the astonishing thing was trying to contact the municipal management at Waterfalls about the dereliction of the bridge, its lack of maintenance and a faded sign that claims that entering the park is at one's own risk. Negligence is not a legal excuse. Neither the tour company nor I – a week later – had received any response to our calls and emails, but the receptionist did return to me my entrance fee when we confronted him once my colleagues had extracted me from the bridge. I am not sure that the Waterfalls receptionist really understood the principle of corporate responsibility. The good news was that I did not feature in the irreverent *1000 Ways to Die* broadcast on DSTV.

BATTLEFIELDS: RETHINKING IDENTITY

Field trips to the KwaZulu-Natal battlefields, on which I was a participant observer during 2017 and 2019, aimed to find out:

- how students learn to learn;
- how students experience the research encounter;
- how students react to different histories (Zulu, British,
  Boer, Indian) in explained relation to each other as they
  clashed on the battlefields; and
- to observe how students make sense of, and live, their field
  experiences.

My analytical frame of reference is *SUBtext*, a student research
magazine in which students, none of them parents, reflected on
their field research. During one three-day excursion during 2019
I watched, listened and connected experiences across a number
of tours. No students were interviewed – or harmed – during this
exercise. No ethical rules were transgressed. The excursion had
been duly authorised by a line manager. The background was that
of cultural policy research, as formulated by class lecturer, Sarah
Gibson, who observes:

> Moving from the United Kingdom to South Africa forced
> me to reflect on what Cultural Studies is as a discipline,
> and what my pedagogical philosophy to teaching is across
> different cultures and contexts. This enabled me to reflect
> on how much of Cultural Studies knowledge, theories
> and methodologies I had previously taught where in fact
> produced in and from the global North. I began to explore
> and conceptualise what a transformed, Africanised and
> decolonised Cultural Studies curriculum should be in the
> context of the global South, as I also reflected on my own
> positionality in the classroom as a white, British teacher.

This resulted in transforming my understanding of the discipline within a South African context (Teaching and Learning Statement, 2019).

CULTURAL POLICY

The Centre for Communication, Media and Society (CCMS) was integral in the development of post-apartheid cultural policy, having been contracted in the early 1990s by the Convention for a Democratic South Africa (CODESA) to work with the Human Sciences Research Council (see Shepperson 1993). Earlier moves towards cultural policy had been spearheaded by African National Congress (ANC) stalwart Mewa Ramgobin (n.d.; see also Tomaselli and Ramgobin 1988). Ramgobin had worked with CCMS in mapping out the basic propositions of an inclusive cultural policy and had implemented his Gandhian principles of (passive) resistance across the Natal province during the late 1980s via the United Democratic Front and the Natal Indian Congress. The student field trips that followed in the late 2000s derive from this earlier mobilising moment that drew heavily on Australian cultural policy theory and practice (see Sterne 2002). Cultural policy did not start with the *Government Gazette* as presented by the 2019 class after the trip, but it resulted from an intensive process of negotiation during the late 1980s and 1990s that included a variety of civic stakeholders, including academics, from across the emergent nation.

The proposal submitted to CODESA was that all monuments should be retained and used for reconciliation (Tomaselli and Mpofu 1997). We needed to be mindful of history. This includes Shaka's bloody domination of previously fragmented Zulu clans, Mzilikazi's breakaway swathe of destruction through the interior, the dispossession of the First People across southern Africa, the Trekkers, the Boers, the British.

The issue, of course, is that history is very complicated and cannot be reduced to binary opposites of 'Us versus Them', though, in contrast, interpretations of history can be very easy. What we suggested for the proposed cultural policy was to generate debate over meanings, issues and solutions. As F.W. de Klerk argued, no one hated Cecil Rhodes more than did Afrikaners, whose Boer republics were destroyed by British imperialism. As Christopher Merrett argues with regard to giving Rhodes a free pass:

> There is every reason why memorials to Rhodes, actual or symbolic, should not form part of the present-day South African landscape. But nor is there justification for unseemly behaviour and unlawful destruction or meaningless rhetoric and sloganeering. It is worth remembering that Rhodes is very much a figure of our times. His entrepreneurial methods would sit easily with modern predatory capitalism and globalisation, with its reliance on cheap labour and deprivation of workers' rights. He would also be comfortable with the vacuous celebrity culture of today, in which people of minimal achievement and overweening mediocrity are elevated to extraordinary and undeserved heights.[1]

Rhodes was allowed to remain unmolested during National Party rule as a sobering reminder of a particular era of exploitation. Simply imposing one historical monologue over others kills the dialectic and simplifies history to the point of farce. Amnesty is conferred when one is made absent. Just as Rhodes, fell, so sculptor Andries Botha's 'soft' King Shaka was removed from the new Durban airport because he was not depicted as warrior-like and Botha's elephant sculpture on entering Durban was initially terminated because it reminded the ANC of Inkatha, the Zulu traditionalist national movement with which it was at war during the 1980s. A statue of Gandhi was also despoiled, as were horses memorialised from the fallen during the First World War. Nelson Mandela also came into the sights of some and the *bittereinder* memorial at the Women's Monument in

Bloemfontein, where 50 000+ Boer women and children and black internees are memorialised, is now protected by razor wire from copper thieves.[2]

WRITING THE WRITE

Field excursions are designed to teach students to rethink history, their place within it and how to mobilise through it. Many students had over the years contributed to *SUBtext* and most who visited Zululand, the Kalahari and elsewhere returned to Durban changed, reinvigorated and with a new sense of identity and of the role of history in shaping our understanding of who we are and how we fit into the world. As Andrew Dicks expresses it:

> History is important because we ... are the sum of all events (the good, the bad and the indifferent) that have happened to us. This sum product guides our actions in the present. This is true for the individual, as well as for society. For example, you would not exist had your parents never met; South Africa would be very different, and might even have gone by a different name had the Dutch settlers never arrived here, followed by the British. The only way we can understand who we are and how we got that way is by learning about the past. Similarly, the only way we can understand others is by learning about their past. If we were ignorant of what made others who they are – in terms of how they think and behave – we would make all sorts of blunders in our interactions with them. Most importantly though, we study the past to understand our mistakes, and to attempt to never make those mistakes again. Historian William Lund sums this up rather well in saying: 'We study the past to understand the present; we understand the present to guide the future.' (Dicks 2014: 10)

In connecting with the future, Abulele Njisane's evocative story on her Zulu identity shifting in terms of her Kalahari field work experience is illustrative. She writes on the unfamiliar that she negotiated in the field in connecting premodernity with postmodernity:

> I remember walking through the dry, long grass and seeing an old worn down building. Suddenly, nothing felt familiar to me, it was like I was a stranger in a foreign land, with people that valued drawings on rocks not only as part of their heritage but also their indigenous identity. They had strong pride in it even though they knew that there are people who say that the ancient people who drew the drawings might not even have been Bushmen. This strong belief in one's identity is the opposite of my environment where my peers embrace technology as part of our daily lives, express our indigeneity in a haphazard and ambiguous way through social networking sites like Facebook, Mxit, and Twitter and where our identity is seen as an individual, commercial and publicised construction of expressing one's self. I realised that this was going to be a life changing, eye opening and informative experience. (Njisane 2012: 4)

Njisane produced this nuanced self-reflection for a magazine that did not earn students study credits. The magazine was not included in the university's work-load spreadsheet and the time spent by staff in producing it, drew no recognition from Authority. It was surplus to time-table requirements. Yet, it was in this magazine that students engagingly negotiated the self and their research in ways that were arresting, relevant and innovative.

PRESENCE/ABSENCE

Waiting/writing on the bus for the class to board for the 2019 KwaZulu-Natal battlefield excursion, I overheard the following: 'I don't remember you from class. Are you registered? First time we've met! Welcome to the course – halfway through the academic year!' These were the remarks made by an adjunct lecturer as 30 honours students boarded the bus for the field trip. 'Dr Livingstone, I presume?' asked one professor, as a previously absent one staggered into the bus. The lecturer turned taking a register into a pedagogical opportunity and she reminded the class that they were on the tour to learn, while a second adjunct lecturer cautioned them on too much partying and the value of early nights. The students complied – mostly.

A roll call was conducted and a WhatsApp group was constituted to keep track of strays at the various remote sites to be studied. We departed one student short. On our return we learned that she had been mugged on her way to campus. Just another day in paradise as we all awaited the promise of President Ramaphosa's 'New Dawn' – as the N3 had become a war zone, with 14 000 articulated trucks having being torched and looted during 2018 and 2019 and 200+ drivers killed by organised xenophobic gangs who are never brought to book. This was the same intercity highway that we were travelling, but fortunately there were no incidents. Mhlongo's composition is pertinent here: 'WRITE! for them [the government, the police, the xenophobics] to read, so they'll understand.'

During the early 2000s, a recurring pattern was that half the undergraduate class was absent all the time, meaning that classes of 400 could be accommodated in classrooms seating just 200. Chronic absenteeism is an indicator of deeper concerns and the ways in which post-millennium students engage the virtual world. Absent and even present students often ask the question: 'Is it (class attendance, a test, an essay) compulsory?' This is the First Law of Student Procrastination. Realising that evasion is not an option, the caveat becomes: 'Is it for marks?' It is at this point that the corollary of the First Law kicks in, especially when lecturers try to respond intelligently and patiently to the First Law and its caveat parroted at them by students.

The corollary states that 'students asking these kinds of questions indicate that all they have learnt is how to write exams.' The Second Law of Procrastination states that students who only know how to write exams have yet to learn how to learn. The lecturer's stock response to these kinds of questions is found in the Law of Irritated Reaction: 'A register will be taken!' – as was done on the bus, with the passengers being counted every time the bus departed. Happily, most students in the 2019 class actually got into learning mode quite quickly. The class presentations the following week were 'for marks' – and all students were handed a peer assessment of group discussions form to fill in. Some students initially failed to offer assessments of their peers, leaving this task to the lecturers! To the rescue, the indomitable adjunct chivvied up the laggards. One absconding group, however, failed to turn up to class to present their project in class. Appropriately, and with semiotic irony, their topic was Fugitives Drift. No apologies, no explanation. No marks. Hopefully, they learned something in the process.

Learning – especially during field trips as in class – is a collective socialisation process. That is why peer marks were part of the assessment, as is hiking in the hot sun. Well, the salaried at Spionkop, the oldest professors (and two very fit female students) reached the steep pinnacle first, followed much later by panting young stragglers being chivvied along by the *agterryers* (after riders) – the two middle-aged female staff members – pushing from the back of the long column snaking up the very steep track. For the next visit I suggested that we set a practical participatory research task for the students: to drag a canon up the side of the Spionkop mountain so that they could experience field conditions first-hand – if without the enemy actually firing at them.

Subjects of non-learning practices just don't know that that they don't know or they don't care that they don't know. And they don't know that they cannot know if they don't know. The lack of self-responsibility occurs when something is 'free' – like education – as was this field trip. Learning needs to be taken seriously. Class participation is necessary. Reading is a not a distraction to partying. One group did inform the report-back class that one of their own was wilfully absent and that the remainder were taking up the slack. Those at the class presentations did know that they were learning. The need for innovation and effort was indicated in the field trip manual that asked students to assess the tourist/heritage sites signage, organisation and visitor friendliness. Most students did make notes, did get involved and did try to connect their theory with the practice at the various sites. This course pack included readings and worksheets that encouraged students to become familiar with the sites visited (all readings aimed at visitor/tourist market, not academic) and to be active while on the field trip, rather than simply being passive tourists sightseeing and bussed around from place to place.

In documenting my thoughts on the bus when we departed, I wrote on my laptop (while the students were singing, sleeping, and/or fixated on their cell phones) that too many students today want the perks but not the education. They want the degree but not the learning. They want the certificate but not the skills. Their skill is 'being absent' and expecting the taxpayer to cover the social costs of their lack of civic and self-responsibility. They want the jobs but without the responsibility. One student wanted chocolate, not the nutritious sandwich and fruit provided in the lunch pack. On employment, they will want their salary without earning it. It is not just the odd exception, it is a recurring pattern. It started in 1994 – the year of political liberation. What also came to pass is, as one adjunct observed:

The lacklustre approach to learning has failed many of us. We are no longer desiring to learn, we study to obtain a certificate in the hope of getting a job; and in many ways, academics are no longer fulfilling their mandate, to actively engage in the learning process as they are bogged down with administrative processes – everything has become a procedure. (Shannon Landers)

As we arrived at the Blood River monument battle site, where the Voortrekkers engaged and defeated a huge Zulu army, a student cynically asked, 'What is this?' This irritated question had followed a lecture by a history professor on the bus on the way to the site and reminded me of Nyasha Mboti's (2012: 10) observation: 'Finding the Other, who is also inside each researcher, is bound up with questions such as "What am I doing here?" and "How did I get here?"' A whole group declined to examine a cairn slightly off the path – because that was not part of their specific project – much to the exasperation of one of their professors. But I noted that the bulk of the class very soon after arrival at the first site started show keen interest, photographing, talking to the Blood River museum curator and each other, asking questions, taking notes, reading panels and engaging with exhibits. Anton, the Blood River site's hospitality officer was highly responsive, whereas the Ncome reception desk barely tolerated the group's interruption of their cell phone addiction, though our Ncome guide did ask us to explain one of the dioramas to him. As Mfundisa Miya observed of her awakening on entering the Duggan-Cronin photographic gallery in Kimberley, which houses the most comprehensive collection of southern African ethnographic photographs from the 1930s:

It really was a surprise to me how I became so enthusiastic about the pictures; I felt I needed to understand the history behind them so I started to read through the captions on the walls. I also found myself taking pictures and linking everything to representation and imaging. Thinking back I laugh at myself at how excited, I got and how I actually enjoyed 'staring' at these marvellous images. (Miya 2013: 1)

This kind of excitement was similarly evident among the 2019 class. Regrettably, however, universities as communal socialisation experiences such as offered by group learning, seminars and field trips are becoming rarer in the era of so-called blended learning, which de-emphasises actual interaction within physical spaces and atomises students and lecturers within massed virtual environments, even more so during the 2020 COVID-19 lockdowns. Interestingly, few students had accessed the Moodle site supporting the course, despite the rhetoric of blended learning being encouraged by universities as the solution to all problems. No use was made of online discussion forums. However, the disposition among most of the students began to change noticeably when they compared Ncome (the Zulu side) with Blood River (the Trekkers' side) having crossed the Bridge of Reconciliation that joined the two adjacent sites on either side of Blood River, which marked the bloody battle in 1838 where 464 Trekkers faced off with 10 000 Zulu warriors.

Once the majority of students got into the dialectical groove, their respectfulness of the exhibits, the curators and the histories depicted shone through. They did not take sides, they did not take umbrage and they did not parrot reductive Fanonesque slogans. They showed empathy no matter who was buried under their feet in the field and commemorated in monuments above these mass graves. Here I am referring mainly to the female students as the males seemed to be nursing hangovers mostly and were so quiet as to be largely invisible. The name 'Jameson' was uttered often, but this was not the Jameson Raid when in 1895 a rag-tag British army unsuccessfully attacked the South African Republic. When fees fall, the whisky of the same pronounced name fills the void. Mainly, the student photographer was active, here, there, everywhere, videoing, interviewing and observing. But his camera was never in your face, though I was nailed for an interview on the second day after I had tried to evade the student's attentions. Now, that's good journalism. That's initiative. That's to be commended. As a chronicler, ethnographer and photographer in the field, one is in documentary and analytical mode 24 hours a day. Historian Donal McCracken further observed when locating King Shaka in history:

> Shaka is important because he forged the Zulu nation thus creating Zulu nationalism which is still alive and well. He never fell out with the whites, but his campaigns against the Swazi and the Pondo are largely airbrushed away under the mantle of the Black Napoleon warring against an invisible enemy. He was an autocrat and like many such could be charming enough and certainly astute enough. That he was assassinated is also not unknown for autocrats. He is certainly an inspiration and in a strange way a vision of hope for African society emerging from apartheid very rapidly and at the same time dealing with the world change. The two together are a great pressure on black society and it is rather ironic the victory of Africa has been at a cultural price which is very high indeed, much more so than the corresponding decline of white society. (email, 25 January 2020)

As Richard Green, who made a movie on the making of the *Shaka Zulu* television series, commented, producer:

> Bill Faure told me that he and the SABC were having a hard time trying to explain why they were spending so much money on a black 'hero'. I made a behind the scenes documentary on the series, which was eventually censored. I was critical of the actors breaking the informal

cultural boycott, and asked them if they had any idea
of what was going on in SA at the time Shaka Zulu was
being filmed. (email 25 January 2020)

When I talk about colonialism of Africa by the Brits, French,
Portuguese, German and Arabs, I tuck in Shaka, to everyone's
surprise. Our colleagues also overlook the brutal English
colonisation of Scotland and Ireland among others, and that
the Sioux sided with the British against white settlers moving
West in the 1700s – but few students are able to understand that
colonisation was not necessarily a skin colour thing.

Njisane, again, intensively reflecting on her Kalahari trip, writes:

I might not remember in detail every aspect of this
trip, but because of photos and the video diaries that
we made every two days, one will be able, through
piecing together things with the help of the fertile
imagination, to go back to that lived experience of
meeting and sharing space with one who is called
the Other [Bushmen]. I might not have understood
it clearly then, but I realised that I had found myself
doing ethnographic work unknowingly. These
encounters have truly triggered a desire for me to
write and express the power of engaging in participant
observation because the idea of difference is bridged
when one engages with what one says is the Other.
After all, culture is indeed a lived experience, a day-to-
day process. Thus to understand someone else's culture
we are required to be observant in the process of what
becomes known as their culture, and which, through
a shared heritage also is our culture. (Njisane 2012: 7)

THE CONTRADICTIONS OF HISTORY

McCracken's lectures exposed the contradictions of shared histories as articulated on the eighteenth- and nineteenth-century battlefields, the always-shifting alliances between Voortrekkers, Zulus and British, and the fact that the British army had Zulu regiments and Indian cohorts, that Zulu and Boer were aligned against the British. Zulus fought other Zulus, Pondos and Swazis also. Within the laager at Blood River were British settlers and black servants. P.W. Botha himself cast the battle as a clash of civilisations rather than as a race war (*Die Vaderland*, 15 December 1981). History is complicated and messy. Zulus and Boers came to respect each other irrespective of the killing of the Piet Retief Voortrekker party and of Blood River in 1838 before the British invasion in 1879. The Voortrekkers actually had little sense of race at that time. In fact 'race' then signified 'nationality', as in English versus Dutch, or French versus Spanish, but not 'black' versus 'white'. However, race-speaking certainly embodied racial ranking of one kind or another. Reductionism that casts relationships as simply binary need be queried for, as Timothy Keegan states:

> There is ... a tendency to reduce South African history to a morality play, in which a long series of calamities and degradations is visited upon the local people by the evil forces of colonialism. There is enough truth in this. But Africans were never passive victims, stripped of agency, and the invasive forces were never omnipotent. (Keegan 1996: 8)

As Dicks (2014) argues, how we view history affects how we construct our own identities and versions of the other. Our students' re-identifications of self were expansive, nuanced and accommodating, though on the 2019 tour, I suspect, a few students did construct themselves as other, not wanting to be there and resenting the continuous and exhausting three-day class. They could skip scheduled two-hour seminars but not the field trip and they could evade the analysis of self-other engagements.

The group presentations the following week were passionate, dynamic, well researched, well illustrated and theorised to a functional degree. Apart from a few reductionist statements borrowed from the less discerning published literature, the students in fact embodied the spirit of South African cultural policy that aims at dialogue, reconciliation and respect for diversity. Interacting historical narratives were engaged with, rather than mechanistic ideological discourses imposed. Trying to understand the experiences and perspectives of the other was a task taken seriously. History is a conversation about interacting interpretations derived from different readings of historical evidence – it is not one story, not one interpretation or just one way of making sense. The students understood that. To cite Mhlongo again: 'Written can be passed on from generation to generation from one to another', and from one class to the next, here it can be further engaged with and analysed (cited in Mbatha 2013: 10).

MAKING SENSE OF THE EXPERIENCE

Ndu Ngcobo summed up the 2014 battlefields excursion in a way that applies to all field trips:

A sense of accomplishment filled the air, the trip had brought theory to life, signs had been deciphered and thanks to the guidance of the professors, what was absent had been uncovered. The art of critical thinking had allowed for the abstract journey of finding a deeper meaning to the various things we encountered than what is readily available on the surface. (Ngcobo 2014: 3)

Finding out about ourselves is another objective, as Brigitte Logie observed of sojourns with desert communities: 'The time away from the cocoon of urban civilization resulted in most of us learning more about ourselves – when we had originally thought we were there to learn about our hosts' (Logie 2011: 3). This was the objective. We could not spend enough time in the field to study sufficiently with hosts, so the Kalahari brief was that students critically examine the nature of the research relationship to learn more about themselves and how their hosts manage the encounters. Shanade Barnabas, who has been a member of my Kalahari research team since 2008, observed:

> What drove me to complete my master's dissertation was not the mountains of books I had to read, nor the hope of academic success, but rather the conviction that my research could make a valuable difference to peoples' lives in this community. Sitting at that seminar and being reminded of all the reasons I began the research helped to stoke the embers of a passion nearly overwhelmed by its own ambitions. What we do here at CCMS can actually make a difference to people's lives. Our research can actually *mean* something. (Barnabas 2011: 9)

The subtext here is that when we squander our opportunities by being absent, disinterested and distracted, we also squander the potential benefits for our hosts, communities and our own society. One Nigerian student who revelled in the field experience, through honours, master's, PhD and later as a post-doctoral student at the University of Johannesburg, Itunu Bodunrin, says:

> The Kalahari experience taught me about Life; how to tolerate and accommodate others in in my personal space. The Kalahari tests patience and tolerance, influenced by both human and environmental factors; by the heat and wind in the mid-day, and by extreme cold at night. I forged strong bonds with my colleagues from CCMS, who came from South Africa, the UK and the US. We joked, cooked, washed dishes and shivered together in the Kalahari cold.

All these were experiences that will forever change my perspective to life. Regardless of the hardships, I have no doubt that I enjoyed every bit of this research/adventure more than these mere words can tell. (Bodunrin 2013: 5)

And, as Lauren Dyll concluded:

The value of the PPCP [private public community partnership] model I generated was recognised by my examiners, and one of them commented that it is: 'an elegant and generalizable model for future PPCP projects ... a workable model that actually can be used by project planners ... This section of the dissertation could be sent directly to the South African government's tourism development office for its immediate use, such is the model's clarity and obvious practicality'. (Dyll 2012: 3)

In fact, this model was applied across southern Africa by a company that manages lodges and sites owned by local communities. So, for me, what the 2019 class has done should be helpful to the cultural policy and heritage sectors if the projects can be made available to them.

To conclude on the value of writing (and reading):

WRITE! oh Africa WRITE!
Write, for it is RIGHT
Let's WRITE for the nations to see
WRITE for them to read, so they'll understand. (Mholongo, cited in Mbatha 2013: 10)

As Shannon Landers observed in a comment in response to this chapter: 'Mhlongo's poem demonstrates the value of the Battlefields trip for our Honours module. If anything, we must write. The past students' excerpts reveal the importance of engaging with what we are learning, if not for the "other" then at least for ourselves.'

A variation of Terman's Law (cited in Martin 1973: 57) states: 'There is no direct relationship between the quality of an educational program and its cost (or the "time" spent doing nothing/something in the classroom).' Active participation in a collective learning environment is the key.

Notes

1. Read more at: https://www.fromthethornveld.co.za/the-empire-strikes-back/#_edn6
2. *Bittereinder*: The diehard Boers who continued fighting even after the end of the Anglo-Boer War

8 Of Colonialism and Capture

Social media notwithstanding, graffiti remains the subversive medium of choice for any true revolutionary, especially if painted on historical buildings and monuments. Forget Twitter and consult the nearest wall. Graffiti on campuses (excluding toilet walls depicting acts that would embarrass *Playboy*) finally exposes the ultimate culprit, an enemy that had been hiding in plain sight and it has infiltrated everywhere. Our rainbow-tinted exuberance suckered us into believing that apartheid had been the enemy, that once we could establish freedom, democracy, black economic empowerment (BEE), the National Economic Development and Labour Council (NEDLAC), the New Partnership for Africa's Development (NEPAD), stricter visa regulations and a non-racial society, everything would be hunky-dory.

Vanguardist campus activists have liberated themselves from false consciousness and exposed the true enemy: colonialism. (This is a one-size-fits all demon that forgets that every society everywhere at every time has been brutally colonised – often successively and always differently.) Transforming from apartheid by tinkering with racial targets was first base, rebuilding and our society was second base, but playing with decolonisation moves us into the big international leagues.

Once decolonisation had replaced HIV as the 'new struggle', the National Development Plan could really build progress because, at root, all ills in settler economies have colonial origins. A Roman Dutch judicial system is alleged by the Zumarites to have undermined government at every turn. The Public Investment Corporation (PIC), the government pension fund, however, broke ranks when it approved the colonisation of the true blue South African Breweries by nasty imperialist, Anheuser-Busch, massively enriching its South African shareholders. This capitalist system is linked to a Westminster 'Parliament' that was alleged to have embarrassed President Zuma while questioning the excesses of Zuptanomics.

The First People in all cape provinces are largely ignored in their pleas that Afrikaans be recognised as an indigenous language. And no one but the Khoi and the San talk about restoring their historical claims to most of southern Africa. If the First People were indeed the first, disagreements over *Homo naledi* notwithstanding, the rest of us are second, third and fourth, eventually to the power of n. The further down the time chain, the fewer rights we should get. In going back this far, the campus decolonisers themselves will need decolonisation. In the United States, the whole point of Trump-o-nomics is to decolonise the United States of good sense, to punish American business gone global, to engage in Big Wall tendrepreneurship and to keep out Latin American narco-colonisers who, unlike the Aztecs' religious sacrifice, simply kill to secure market share. Xenophobia and markets know no bounds, whether in Gauteng or anywhere else.

In the modern world, animals are confined to reserves, cages, hunted, branded, milked and are bought and sold, just like slaves. Viruses often emerge from such mistreatment, as did COVID-19 and most viruses that preceded it. Animals are assumed to lack affective capacity – even as our dogs welcome us home, lick us, paw us and lie with us. Anyone who reads Lawrence Anthony's book *The Elephant Whisperer* (2009) cannot but be astonished at our dualistic human narrow-mindedness that prevents most humans from entering into the metaphysical realms of animals, as crazy as this sounds. It is only crazy because contemporary conventional science has no way to explain it, to verify it, or to mathematise it. Also, many who proselytise such encounters often come across as being a little dotty. However, 'crazy' is a relative term, culturally specific and neurologically indeterminate. Hearing voices may be diagnosed as schizophrenia by modern psychiatry, but as the voices of ancestors or ghosts by subjects of different ontological frameworks.

To the north, war veterans proved under Mad Bob Mugabe that the ultimate victory against colonialism was the eradication of currency itself, returning to bartering practices. Unleashing the anti-colonial Genie makes the very concept of Gini a moot point. Without currency, it is impossible to measure Gini-coefficients. The outcome is to return to a state of timeless nature and ultimate freedom from the yokes of colonialism, imperialism, neoliberalism and capitalism – just as the sunny sanitised tourist brochures represent mythical and timeless 'Africa'. This romantic image persists, even as the killers of currency drive through and over their inconvenient serfs, in their bulletproof sedans imported from Europe and protected by armed troop carriers and phalanxes of aggressive bodyguards armed with imported Russian weapons. This great victory, claim these obnoxious politicians or People of Worth (PoW), has restored the dignity of the poorest of the poor. The obverse, of course, is that the richest of the rich shop in Europe, get medical treatment in Singapore and buy property unaffordable to anyone else in the Western Cape. The elite will have stashed their goodies behind fortified compounds and in Swiss banks while exempting themselves from global institutions of accountability. Zvakanyorwa Sadomba (2011) identifies the conundrum. Zimbabwe's revolution sets a new agenda and raises anew the intriguing question: 'What are the people of Africa trying to free themselves from and what are they trying to establish?'

While we try to figure this out, the world moves on. Europe and Turkey have absorbed millions of refugees from the Middle East and North Africa. South Africa resents the thousands crossing the Limpopo and xenophobia is re-emerging everywhere. Colonialism, put back on the agenda in 2017 by the inimitable Helen Zille who, like Donald Trump, confuses tweeting with hard policy (Saunderson-Meyer 2017). The trumpeters' compulsion to the issuing of shorthand insults via Twitter might have resulted in a world war. Rash statements commonly draw forth rage, retribution and revenge. Is it not better to write boring, impenetrable and philosophical exegeses that argue the point methodologically and theoretically with supporting references? Studiousness requires irrelevance, well ensured by the time that publication is secured. That is the value of academia. Takes forever. Much safer. Rhetoric, argumentation and thoughtfulness, and a consideration for the consequences of ill-advised ravings, must be taken into account. Think, theorise and then teach – the three Ts.

When I first visited Ghana in 1994, I met President Jerry Rawlins and folks from across Africa participating in the African Council for Communication Education (ACCE) conference. We South Africans were the flavour of the moment. Heroes all, we were welcomed into the African fold, and immediately educated on the lamentable failure of colonialism in West Africa, in contrast to its perceived success in eastern and southern Africa. This was expressed in the recurring epithet, 'The British did not take West Africa seriously enough.'

'Eh?' muttered the South African delegates. Our newfound African colleagues pointed to road, rail, port and civil infrastructures, civic institutions and functioning rules and regulations. These, they observed, had outlasted the departure from eastern and southern Africa of those groups labelled by sloganeering students as our 'colonial masters'. If they were our masters, why did they leave? Did the kids become too unruly? If so, then the relationship was never fully a master-servant one. That is what the sizable South African contingent in Accra signified. Repression is never complete. Resistance is always underway. Democracy is always bubbling, if under the surface. The 'masters' are never fully in control – even if, as Zille suggested, with reference to the history of Singapore, 'colonialism was not all bad'. Decolonisation, however, requires the destruction of the colonial infrastructure and is systematically delivered by the burning of campuses and schools, trains and bankrupting state-owned enterprises (SOEs) via the application of Zuptanomics, also known as state capture (by gangsters and criminals), so that we can, with restored dignity, claim our illusive freedom.

While in Ghana I found myself in the president's limousine, loaned to the conference to speed up organisational arrangements. His chauffer was allowed to drive on the wrong side of the road to escape the interminable traffic jams on decaying single lane arterial roads. Quite scary. I doubt that the car even had a blue light and there was no noisy, speeding and aggressive cavalcade of self-important VIP security sirens within which our own presidents and politicians wrap themselves. The wrong side of the road privilege was accorded to Rawlins's car only. In Johannesburg, most taxis think that they are part of Rawlins's entourage as they are often on the wrong side and red lights mean little. Stop streets are ignored by everyone. The Arrive Alive campaign means nothing. Arriving dead seems to be the objective in Johannesburg. Since Rawlins's limousine was the only one allowed on the wrong side, all motorists knew that it would not be followed by phalanxes of reckless opportunists riding in its slipstream. No Twitter in Rawlins's day, but when he spoke off script at the opening of the conference, the Ghanaian media turned the microphones off. They missed the real news.

Oh, and what of colonialism, whether British, Arabic, Portuguese, Spanish, Dutch, Japanese, Scandinavian, or Russian? Some benefits were that folks learned to write, read and do maths. It also generated resistance and helped to forge national identities and new nations across the globe. But mostly, European colonialism's most significant import was Christianity, whether of the theological or happy-clappy kind. Zille's erstwhile nemesis, Pastor Mmusi Maimane, owed his religion, his suit and his political position as leader of the opposition to our British colonial heritage, rather than his tribal inheritance. By temporarily suspending the seemingly colonial-supporting Zille from the party, the Democratic Alliance (DA) ironically projected an image of a black anti-colonial party in a state that was being captured by the new colonisers: a corrupt comprador bourgeoisie enabled by the Zuptas, the Russian nuclear industry and the South African National Roads Agency, the highway robbers legitimised behind e-tag tolling. We ceded our economy to foreign interests that will indebt us forever. There can be nothing good in this form of colonialism – comprador monopoly capital – that stole and destroyed local infrastructure, ruined the economy and indebted the Treasury in perpetuity.

I do not participate in the Twittersphere. Too many hashtags, truncated philosophers and people who have lost their jobs or have been fined or imprisoned for their rants.

DEMOCRACY AND LOSING

South Africa becomes more Monty Pythonesque every day. When in 2015 the Springboks first lost to minnows, Japan, during the Rugby World Cup, the sports scribes complained about the faulty game plan and player fatigue. But the politicians' characteristic riposte was to demand the selection of more black players. The zany logic seems to be: if we are going to lose, we might as well lose 'democratically'; i.e., via racially representative sides selected by a political committee that knows nothing about sport. Bafana Bafana's dismal record has revealed that 100 per cent black racial representation is not needed to lose consistently. We lose because we have become a loser nation. Losing is now part of our victimological DNA.

In the 1990s we were a winning nation. We won democracy, we won the hearts of the world, we won the 1995 Rugby World Cup and we won (with a bit of hanky-panky) the 2010 Soccer World Cut bid, even as Bafana failed. We won our dignity, restored freedom of speech and debated comprehensive visions and missions. We worked for the dream of democracy, non-racialism and inclusion.

The immediate post-liberation state generated Africa's leading economy and a welfare system bar none. Despite chronic underfunding, and the annual attacks on educational infrastructure from 2017 onwards, South Africa has retained five universities in the global top 500 and millions of students want education. And, as became clear during the COVID-19 pandemic, mandatory tuberculosis vaccination and the government's fast response may have partly shielded South Africa from the worst effects of the virus. South Africa is one of the few countries to require this prophylaxis, in contrast to Italy, Spain and the United States, which were hardest hit.

Yet the prevailing myth is that nothing has changed.

To transform rugby, as an example, the South African Rugby Union started with intergenerational development at school level, not with BEE scorecards so beloved by politicians. South Africa won the 2019 World Cup under the leadership of its first black captain. Success has to be nurtured from the bottom up, as was effected by rugby – as was liberation that took over a century to effect. Having liberated ourselves, we now imprison ourselves in short-term thinking and opportunistic discourses of entitlement – we want, but we don't want to work for what we think liberation owes us. We destroy what we build and we rebuild what has been destroyed – all in the name of transformation.

As one of my hashtag-savvy correspondents observes: 'My perception is that the "born free" generation has spawned a faction of black students whose extreme racial views baffle former black activists who fought for non-racialism.' The #transformation activists claim that the former 'liberal' institutions are racist and that they remain uncomfortable and marginalised on campus due to 'structural' or 'institutionalised' racism or a 'Eurocentric' outlook and curriculum.

The (exclusively black) student experience at the universities of Venda, Limpopo, Zululand and Walter Sisulu, where the curriculum often remains Eurocentric, does not attract a hashtag because of their faculty profile. At the multiracial city universities students are predominantly middle class, while at the rural campuses they are mainly lumpenproletariat. Is it any wonder, then, that the eminent French critical scholar Manual Castells wryly observed that 'transformation' is a word that South Africans use when they stop thinking and start making conversation over a glass of wine (see Cloete 2015)? Are the whiners like wine drinkers – characters in a Monty Python satire?

Does transformation hinge on claiming that an inexorable pre-given white racist institutional culture exists and that blacks must necessarily hail themselves as perpetual victims? Under such circumstances, neither 'transformation' nor 'decolonisation' can ever be completed. Has the architect of apartheid, Hendrik Verwoerd, been proven correct and Frantz Fanon wrong? God forbid. Below is my experience of the Pythonesque contradictions that arise.

BORDERS I HAVE KNOWN

We lost the University of Witwatersrand's (Wits) Eddie Webster on the South African side of the border into Lesotho in 1979. His name was on a Security Branch 'control list'. The lefties were travelling to a sociology conference in Maseru. On the way back, we – myself, my wife Ruth (then a Wits master's student) and Tony Seeber, an economics lecturer from the University of South Africa (Unisa) – were stopped and our boot was unpacked by some black policemen. They found stacks of printed conference papers, all of which were confiscated. We were interrogated for five hours. In the charge office the polite Afrikaans-speaking Security Branch officer stacked the three sets of papers on his desk and set about reading them while we observed him. Titles with 'black', 'South Africa' or 'apartheid' grabbed his attention. On occasion, he asked for explanations of particular passages. We did not then understand why Seeber was so agitated. He had assured us that he did not have banned materials on him. He paced back and forth like a caged lion.

Of particular interest to the Security Branch officer was Drew Archibald's paper, "The Relevance of Parsons Theory for South Africa'. Actually it had no relevance, but structural functionalism was Drew's forte, drummed into us when we had been undergraduate Wits students ten years earlier. The paper's *lack* of anti-apartheid content intrigued the Security Branch man. He was perturbed that he could not find it. No matter, Ruth said mischievously, have a look at the other copy of the same paper, 'Maybe it moved there.'

Some years later I got stopped again, this time on the way back from an education workshop held in Botswana. In my car was an education lecturer from the Johannesburg College of Education. The lecturer, against my instruction to airmail to South Africa incriminating documents, was found with a *Staffrider* magazine containing a banned poem. The hapless lecturer had an English name, long black hair, smoked a pipe, wore blue jeans, and clearly had no previous experience of being interrogated by impatient young Security Branch officers who harassed us ceaselessly for twelve hours. The lecturer fitted the stereotype; he must be the nervous, hidden communist among us, the Security Branch concluded. Playwrights Benji Francis and Ramadan Suleman were also part of the unfolding charade, vaguely explaining why their performance troupe had a huge chain in their van. The chain was a metaphorical prop – 'We shall break loose from our chains'. The Security Branch never did understand metaphors, so they kept asking about the chain. Neither could they abide the fact that we all made a point of drinking from the same two-litre bottle of Coke, the only refreshment we had. A month later I was told by the Security Branch to pick up the documents (including toilet paper that they had vigilantly numbered) from the local office.

We had been spared the attentions of the same border post a year earlier when we had been at the Botswana Culture and Resistance

Conference, where exiles and internals noisily interacted. This was because, unlike Seeber whom I later learned was a communist (unlike the lecturer, who just looked like communist), our one-year-old son who was with us could not possibly be a communist. The packet of dirty nappies that Ruth proudly waved under the noses of the black border policemen was our passport to a quick transit. Others transiting from Botswana did not have it so easy.

At the same time the Ciskei got its 'independence'. Our group was travelling to Transkei University to participate in a conference there. On the way through the Ciskei the police directed us to a small building that turned out to be a new border post. There the officer demanded our passports/identity books and then stamped them upside down, asking us our names and to whom the documents belonged. The world of apartheid was indeed topsy-turvy.

This reminds me of a Jonathan Jansen story. On arriving at Amsterdam airport for an annual board meeting called by a Dutch research support organisation, of which he was chair, he was asked by a passport officer, 'Now, my good man, what is your business in the Netherlands?' As you can imagine, this officer got a history lesson about the Dutch occupation of the Cape in 1652 – no passports, permission or permits required. Had Jan van Riebeeck been asked his business on setting first foot on the southern shore of Africa, history might have been quite different.

LEARNERS AND LEARNING

When I was at school during the mid-1950s and 1960s, we were called 'pupils', but more often just 'schoolchildren'. Now these youngsters are 'learners'. This semantic engineering does not, of course, conceal the fact that only quarter or so of any undergraduate class actually learns anything substantive, or learns how to learn in the process. The majority simply learn how to write exams and how to manoeuvre through their degree without learning very much at all.

Those who have learned to be helpless are all around us. Fordist edu-factories teach this passive, dependent and debilitating condition. Entertaining the masses is now the job of lecturers where students enrolled at taxpayers' expense think that *they* are clients paying for a product. This instrumentalist attitude is the kiss of death as far as critical thinking is concerned.

Honours student Gail Robinson (2010) debated an article published by a deputy vice-chancellor of teaching and learning, a new Finagle factor, where terms like 'upskill' and 'teachers bridging gaps' were invoked. This language sat uneasily with the research discourse that emanated from other sectors of the university. The polarisation of the argument between 'teaching', on the one hand, and 'research', on the other, often forgets that the best researchers are also often the best teachers. This is because researchers educate from practices in the field, from direct experience, from the empirical and theoretical fronts, so to speak. Good researchers/educators critique the textbooks – a positively unsettling experience for students. Theory and method come alive in the actual practice of the discipline – made possible by research-led education.

Researchers (and, indeed, activists or anyone who is socially involved) engage with students via methods designed to break dependency, replace passivity and promote agency. Regrettably, the word 'teaching' suggests that it is the lecturer who does the work while students passively respond – waiting for the 'service' (as discussed by Brenden Gray in Chapter 4).

Students learn best when they are educating themselves. The 'teacher' is basically the facilitator/educator. The educator should be asking questions, not delivering answers, uploading notes and PowerPoint presentations on Moodle and Blackboard, creating a day-care environment. In the United States during the 1980s and 1990s I learned the Socratic method: ask questions in class and encourage students to debate answers. This method can be a really daunting experience for even the best of educators. Trying to elicit productive debate from often sullen and underprepared students (even from the minority who actually come to class) takes a trial lawyer-like doggedness.

Learning is a dynamic negotiation in the thick of things. This is known as critical pedagogy à la Paulo Freire (2005).

How to cope with Africa and its challenges is discussed next.

GRUMPY STUDIES

One of my regular correspondents, Dave Coplan, a Wits Anthropology professor, pleaded with me not to become another [name of well-known history professor]: 'I do this by loving Africa for what is loveable about it, shrugging off the rest. And every year I make the same New Year's resolution: I will not become a grumpy old white man', wrote the grumpy (now retired) old man. Eric Louw, an arch grump with a keen sense of humour, now at Queensland University, suggested a whole new area of study. Modules could explore: (a) why old people are grumpy with today's world; (b) why white South Africans are grumpy; and (c) why men are grumpy in general.

Then the lecturer could examine why: (a) young people (varsity students) are grumpy with old people (old academics); (b) black people are grumpy with white people; and (c) chauvinists are grumpy with everyone. From this might emerge a new sub-genre of popular culture called 'Grumpy Studies'. This postmodern nonsense could complement aspirational electives like 'The Kardashians and Celebrity Culture'. Guess which one would get the humanities students? Lazy lecturers may not want to teach such modules – just more workload data to enter – but the upside is that they would now have institutional permission to watch such reality television shows during working hours.

Academics get grumpy with students when they produce howlers like: 'Despite the election promise of the ANC [African National

Congress] of a better life for all, the number of South Africans leaving in poverty is growing.' As sociologist Malcolm Draper mischievously observed: 'This cannot be true since poor South Africans have nowhere to go except to jail or to their death. Our neighbours are even poorer and come here to try and escape poverty.' Student howlers like the one commented on by Draper are becoming part of the new journalism.

DOING AND GROOMING

Two decades ago, a study conducted by journalism professor Graeme Addison revealed that South African journalism students do not read newspapers, media students do not watch television and film students do not go to the movies (cited in Greer 1999). Specifically, journalism students do not know how to craft a narrative or proofread copy; they rarely follow current affairs and they do not know that they do not know. Well, the professor left the academy and took tourists white-water rafting. The river froth was exhilarating, rather than irritating, as is the froth in the academy.

Acerbic columnist David Bullard, who usually goes where no one has gone before, argues that if one wants to be an equal opportunity hack, a degree is not necessary. Students and graduates who assume that the certificate overshadows an ability to 'do' are really deluding themselves. That is why doing (the practice) should be linked to studies (understanding the conceptual context). No matter, journalism schools have their place and dismissive columnists have their place also. They keep academics on their toes. What universities are supposed to do is teach students to THINK, to explain how the world works and to solve problems from first principles. Some of the best explainers of how the world works and the implications thereof have been columnists like Raymond Louw, Allister Sparks, William Saunderson-Meyer, Ferial Haffajee, Imraan Buccus, Barney Mthombothi, Ann Crotty and Max du Preez, among others. These folks can both think and write, and thus communicate well – whether or not they have degrees.

Journalism lecturer Marc Caldwell responded to Bullard's denigration of degrees thus:

> I use columns like Bullard's to caution our students who really do think that a degree is everything, that practice is nothing. Many students globally nowadays often think that the world will come to them rather than them going into the world. That's one of the consequences of mobile media – it does come to them. There is no substitute for professional practice, however.
>
> I generally believe that if you can't THINK, then you can't write.
>
> Likewise, as reading is THINKING WITH A TOOL, if you can't think, you can't read.
>
> Our students can neither write nor read. Why?
>
> At UKZN [University of KwaZulu-Natal], students with poor writing skills are sent to The Writing Place, where they 'learn to write'.
>
> But we still fail to put students in contexts where THEY learn to think (swotting for exams is not thinking).
>
> If you MAKE THEM THINK, you're accused of 'teaching philosophy'.
>
> Bullard's view confirms my own on Practice Theory, Situated Cognition and other concepts currently used in sound education theory.

Knowing how to do is just as important as learning what needs to be known. A certificate is not proof enough to get a job. But often, students do not know how to do, what to do, or why they are doing it. Many just learn reams of jargon, which they spew back uncomprehendingly in exam papers and essays. Filling up paper is the objective rather than constructing, arguing, analysing.

'Doing' is, however, what employers look for. The certificate simply signifies that graduates have done time, paid their fees and somehow manoeuvred through a degree. This has been a long-standing problem for the academy. Philosopher Gilbert Ryle (1963) argues that *knowing how* is conceptually distinct from *knowing that*. The object of his argument is the standing of Cartesian ontology. If Ryle were to observe students today, he would find living proof that his contention is absolutely true.

Doing, building experience, developing a portfolio is rarely on the minds of humanities students. When I taught first year I would ask a new class of 300 why they were studying media. The answers were revealing: some wanted to be journalists, mistakenly assuming that this declining sector was well paid. Others wanted the glamour of television exposure, not realising that the average production day is ten hours of exhausting work. None had a camera, even if their uncles did, or had even made a home movie. The remainder mentioned advertising. None believed me that this sector is the most demanding and that such is the stress and work load that eighteen-hour days are the norm. They became sullen when told that it was my job to prepare them for the unrelenting demands of the profession. So we push, pull, cajole and encourage students to get involved in campus media, off- and on-campus internships, to actually meet the industry. For us, that is the hard work; getting the degree conferred is relatively easy.

A textbook publisher warned us that students nowadays cannot concentrate for long periods, are narcissistic and self-absorbed: 'They don't read, they can't write, and they are unable to think critically.' The publisher provided us with case studies analysing this kind of helpless self-centred student. This was our readership, we were told at a workshop. 'Find the formula to connect with this generation of lost souls and the book will be published.'

In Ryle's terms, what do students do, if they are not actually doing? Students don't even behave like students anymore. It is the disruptive rent-a-crowd that cause campus closures who pretend to be students. It is the latter who have a mission, where the former simply have fashion. They preen and strut about as if the much-practised, unnatural, laid-back modelling walk on fashion television is natural. Like platform models, however, they are going nowhere – in an endless loop back to the dressing room. The fashionistas would appear to be a microcosm of the broader society where conspicuous consumption and flaunting of wealth – or just the image of it – has become the norm. Creatively designed masks made for the COVID-19 lockdowns similarly became fashion statements, except in the United States, where wearing a mask marked one as a Democrat, doing the work of the beast.

9 Cartoons, Blackface and Social Critique

Word once reached the College of Humanities that some of our colleagues in the hard sciences were concerned about some of the fluffy thesis titles that were emanating from our part of the academic world. Not scholarly enough, we were told.

This complaint was co-incident with a 2013 Amnesty International seminar on the topic 'Cartooning and the Protection of State Information Act'. Host Ruth Teer-Tomaselli took the audience on a historical, theoretical and methodological journey of the role played by cartoons in enhancing the public sphere, ensuring debate and protecting the democratic dialectic. No fluff here, as entertaining as the talk was. Cartoonist Brandan Reynolds followed with case studies deriving from his own work for *Business Day*, *Weekend Argus* and *Rapport* and, later, the *Sunday Times*.[1]

Jacob Zuma, of course, was the archetypal caricature. Zapiro's sliding vertical showerhead has entered into pan-African folklore.[2] The cartoonist was continuously fending off court actions lodged against him by the president. In solidarity, 28 South African cartoonists banded together in a shared theme to remember Black Tuesday in 1977 when black-targeted newspapers were banned, and Black Wednesday, the day that the Protection of State Information Act was passed by Parliament in 2012.

Looking at this corpus of unfolding history is a chilling reminder of how easily democracy can go wrong and presidents led astray. With but a few squiggles and brevity of words, cartoonists are able to generate objects on which PhDs have been written. Cartoon discourses, their economy of signs and the capturing of prevailing social sentiment speak both literally and symbolically. Analyses that cannot be made in words for fear of legal action are generally permissible in this visual form. Cartoon images might be interpreted by some as 'fluff', but cartoonists' arguments go to the core of the public sphere.

For non-scientists, science-type titles are incomprehensible, but we do not make fun of them. For example, 'Hypercarnivory, Durophagy or Generalised Carnivory in the Mio-Pliocene Hyaenids of South Africa' (Hartstone-Rose and Stynder 2013). Apart from the prepositions, I recognise only two of six scientific terms in this twelve-word title. No matter, the article itself was quite readable.

The humanities deal with humans who actually do the interpreting, whether they are scientists, engineers or accountants. Indeed, it is scientists who devised ways of seeing that was once considered 'fluff' by their own communities: gravity, relativity theory, uncertainty principle and so on. What is fluff or science fiction today is hard science tomorrow. Just watch the Discovery Channel and its endless programmes tracking ever-elusive extra-terrestrials. Like our deans and the People of Worth (PoW) parallel dimensions, they are usually in hiding!

Cartoonists are like bees. They pollinate public discourse and when their pens are made silent, the public sphere will die. As Einstein once said: 'If the bee disappeared off the face of the earth, man would only have four years left to live.' That is no joke.

But when is a joke not a joke?

STORM IN A T-SHIRT

'When I make a law, people think it's a joke, but when I make a joke, people think it's a law.' This was Piet Koornhof's trademark public speech opening. I was reminded of this National Party minister's musings when, after returning home from a month's travelling overseas, I was reading through back copies of some Durban newspapers.

Not much happens in Durban. Only after I left the University of the Witwatersrand (Wits) in early 1981 to work at Rhodes University did I realise that there is a whole world out there where things do happen. But Durban events rarely make the national press.

So, what was the big Durban news? In November 2014, some scholars at Westville Boys High School (WBHS) got stick from a provincial politician. They had not trashed the school or stolen its computers. They had not abused their teachers, strewn the road with burning tyres or attacked road users. They were not drunk, high or misbehaving. Rather, these were art students who had designed some mildly satirical T-shirt images. One of them was of our comical president at the time, Zuma, a visual take on an early poster of Baker's Biscuits, where his bald head and baker's coat was anchored with the label 'Fakers'.[3]

Well, now, seeing the poster on display, the ideologue screamed racism. He published a lengthy column in a Durban newspaper and set a cat among the pigeons. All and sundry were soon commenting on the matter and newspaper letter editors never had it so good. Here, the politician wanted to create a law to censor a joke (in this case, satire). At least old Piet had a sense of humour – and later a Damascus experience when he joined his old foe, the African National Congress (ANC), but only after it had lost its sense of humour. In any event, much sensible debate ensued in Durban's stable of daily newspapers, largely characterised by their syndication greyness. Durbanites finally had a topic to talk about – apart from political hit squads, crime and corruption. Nevertheless, things can get out of control, such as when South African Breweries objected to Justin Nurse's Black Label beer parody, a T-shirt parodying the brand with its slogan altered to read 'Black Labour, White Guilt.[4] I don't recall any ANC ideologues then accusing Nurse of being racist.

WBHS, better known for its cricket and rugby, found itself at the centre of the local public sphere. Simultaneously, Zapiro, in his indomitable way, managed to irritate Hindus by lampooning one of their deities. This was the parallel story in a province with the largest Indian diaspora anywhere. The artists at WBHS were obviously in good company with Zapiro as, like him, they sensibly refrained from commenting on their art or the furore that ensued. Or maybe the Department of Education had imposed silence on the school?

November is also the Diwali firecracker season when opposing sides snap at each other when terrified, shellshocked dogs make straight for the SPCA. While the debates rage about whether or not firecrackers are socially or dog inconsiderate or have any religious significance, the WBHS Faker poster display struck a chord in the same month that the revised and equally contested Protection of State Information Bill landed on President Zuma's desk for signing. I proposed a Protection of Cartoonists Act, to ensure the integrity of the public sphere. These jokers need legal protection from politicians who cannot read irony and who mistake parody (the joke) for defamation (a legal action). The Bill was never signed. Zuma had become a parody of himself.

And, now, for a Norwegian cartoon digression.

VISAS AND TRAVELS

Once upon a time, anyone could go anywhere. The original First People (San) did not need visas to populate the world. The traces of their DNA are everywhere. Their migrations were largely peaceful. In contrast, the Romans, Alexander, Attila the Hun and the Vikings, the Spanish, the French and the English murdered and plundered across the world, destroying civilisations and spreading disease. Everyone colonised everyone else. Colonisation and conquest was the norm. Africa was not the exception.

These thoughts came to mind when I was applying for a visa to visit Fortress Europe. It was 2012 and my trip involved a lecture tour in Norway, speaking at six universities and being accommodated by four. One night in my two-week itinerary was unaccounted for hotel-wise. The Embassy refused to issue a visa until all my bookings for every night were confirmed and proof of payment provided. This was in addition to my paid-for air tickets, three months of bank account statements, my shareholding portfolio, travel and medical insurance and letters of invitation, not to mention my letter of employment and my Scout's honour assurance that I would return to South Africa.

Not wanting to slave each and every hour of my travels to a predetermined schedule, I responded that I would buy an overnight ticket at the station next to the Oslo hotel that I was booked into by Oslo University – the same one at which Nobel laureates are accommodated. Not possible! So I explained that I would take a day train and stay an extra night in Oslo with my host, a professor who, via Norwegian Agency for Development Cooperation, had invested millions in academic projects across southern Africa. He wrote me a formal letter on a departmental letterhead addressed to the Embassy.

Almost immediately, I received from the Embassy a five-page form that my host was instructed to fill in personally. Among the conditions listed were: (a) he was personally responsible for repatriating me in the event that I overstayed, got sick or died and (b) he needed to take the form in person to his local friendly police commissioner to get official clearance for me to stay with him for one night. Now, remember, this was Norway, not apartheid South Africa, Nazi Germany or North Korea.

Helge Rønning blew a fuse, as I knew he would. He called the Embassy and enquired about these conditions – Schengen requirements he was told.

When I arrived in Oslo, all my hosts there were largely disbelieving. They surmised that this was unintentially offensive European Union officialese to which Norway had reluctantly succumbed. Norway would not behave like this otherwise. Rønning even published newspaper comment on the nice, friendly police state that Norway had become since 9/11.

One of my hosts, anthropologist Sidsel Saugestad, gave me a cartoon book called *How to Understand and Use a Norwegian: A User's Manual and Troubleshooters Guide*. It is a wonderfully depreciating take on a people who were travelling on skis and gave off the faint odour of fish until the discovery of North Sea oil made them rich just a few decades ago. The Norwegian, according to this book, is a really quirky character, a loner, someone who rarely speaks because, apart from family, there is no one to talk to in the vast snowy plains, glaciers and mountains.

On my first arrival in Olso in 1992, other than the passport officer and prior to baggage claim, the first Norwegian I encountered was a short man, almost a cartoonish caricature character, with a backpack wearing traditional Norwegian dress, as if for a solitary and bracing mountain walk. He appeared to be waiting for someone. This caricature struck up a conversation with me and then showed me into a room while flashing his identity card at me. He wanted me to unpack my backpack. I imagined – as in Nigeria – that this must be a scam and I told him to buzz off. But he really was an undercover cop and he really did want to pry into my backpack. And he was also really quite pleased that he did not find any contraband. No corruption in this state; the cop did not ask me what I could do for him and wished me good travels. Norway is egalitarian – no one has a sense of entitlement and the king is above reproach.

Unless on an American or European Union passport, one's carefree back packing days are gone. The traveller's every hour is managed by embassies, electronic surveillance (both commercial and state) and police clearances and comic experiences.

GLOBALISATION, VISAS AND TRAUMA

Many of my colleagues gabble on about globalisation. The only organism that was globalising during 2020 was the COVID-19 virus. Yet, television dramas routinely show their characters jetting off across the world without the need for visas, queuing for visas at embassies, being sent off by officials to get yet more documentation, returning to stand in yet more lengthy queues, getting again yelled at by stressed consulate officials, and paying extortionate rates for the application. Then waiting for three weeks for their passports to be processed.

Sometimes securing a visa can take multiple hours of form filling and, stupidly, is the carbon-emitting requirement by many countries that applicants turn up personally at embassies for biometric surveillance and proof of existence. Apart from Australia, which does the process electronically without even holding one's passport, the rest of the world remains in the Dark Ages. Actually, it is the age of modernity that is the problem, as the Dark Ages never required anyone to have passports or to get permission from their employers to travel and no one insisted on travel insurance and return tickets, bank statements or proof of financial probity.

Genghis Kahn had nothing on an Italian embassy official I had to endure in Washington, DC in 1990 when I was returning to Durban from a sabbatical. I was enquiring about a day pass on a stopover in Rome. Followed by two minions, a fearsome female Godzilla ranted and raved at all the folks in the waiting room, demanding to know why they wanted to visit Italy. We were all evicted from the embassy – and those who seemed to be North African got the brunt of her ire. When I arrived in Rome, on applying for a day visa at the airport, I was interrogated by a police officer on why I could not speak fluent Italian. Sounds like home!

I have already commented on my experience with the Norwegian embassy. Now South Africa has surpassed this insanity with own. It's tit for tat. That's what the prominent notice stated in the Russian embassy in Pretoria in 2016, before it lifted visa requirements a year later. Russia treats South Africans in the same way they treat us, said the notice. With contempt. One would think that the BRICS (Brazil, Russia, India, China and South Africa) countries would have eased up on the humiliating visa ritual. Three times I had to evade the e-tolls and observe the mad and disorientated Gauteng drivers invading the endless uncompleted roadworks by bulldozing their own detours around Steyn City, a gated monstrosity, which was built smack in the middle of a previously operating major highway. Much like in Nairobi, and with no signs, no traffic police or any warning, motorists hack through a myriad of self-made muddy tracks trying to find the detour to the route to Pretoria.

Inside in the embassy, we all had to deal with polite and sometimes seemingly impolite officials who were mystified as to why the documentation our respective hosts had sent them could not be found. Mentions were made of telex reference numbers (remember that technology?) and emails taking three days to arrive, and so on. Original paper invitations were expected by courier from one ministry or other. One Russian official was exceedingly polite, while the other barked, yelled and commanded, all the while gesticulating wildly. He was not being rude, that's perhaps the stereotypical Russian way. Or maybe he had watched too many Hollywood movies with Russian characters?

Getting a visa for the United Kingdom is worse, even if the agents bristle with barely concealed polite officiousness. The last time I went to get a visa (in 2013) the new agent was in Overpoort. It did not start well. My appointment for an 'interview' was 11 a.m. At 10.30 a.m., I received a call from a shopper who told me that she had found my passport pack on a ledge at the centre. Was it mine? Having recovered from my astonishment, I asked her to take them to my visa agent on the fifth floor who had lost them in the first place. When I arrived, the building was under reconstruction and I could not find the lifts. Having finally been taken there by a guard, I walked slap-bang out of the lift into throngs of bewildered visa applicants all milling about in the corridor, waiting for their 9 a.m. interviews. I struggled through this mass and found the visa agent, who was unrepentant about losing my documents. I then scrummed my way into the consulate's agent offices, where, in front of everyone (standing, seated, muttering) I declared loudly that I had arrived for my 11 a.m. appointment. I was told by the officials to get to the back of the queue, that is go back in time to 8.30 a.m., which snaked along the outside corridor and down the stairwell. My response was to offer a short tutorial on Britishness and punctuality – theirs. This raised applause from inside the seated massed would-be travelers and their muttering got louder, especially when I queried their extortionate fee from the country that made the Empire so rich during colonial times.

Fearing the beginnings of a riot, I was whisked away into a booth, fingerprinted, eye-printed and printed in every which way. I then gave another tutorial on the unfairness of queue-jumping and was whisked out lest the applause develop into a full-blown riot. My subsequent entry on the consulate agent's website inviting customer experience did not even merit an acknowledgement. So much for British efficiency, fair play and level playing grounds. No wonder mad cow disease is a homegrown British malady. That was my last and final visit to the United Kingdom. I prefer the South African cows.

The Ethiopians have the right idea. They mix extortion with efficiency and pragmatism. Unlike South Africa's Home Affairs, which has been known to jail incoming billionaire investors because they did not have sufficient blank pages (sic), the Ethiopians herd visa-seekers into a room on disembarkation: (i) show your passport here, (ii) they stick the visa into the passport over a previous one if out of date, (iii) pay your US dollars at the next station, (iv) exit to the passport officer, then (v) to baggage, then (vi) scanning, and then exit. Then, if you are in luck, get mobbed, as at most African airports, by a mob of screaming, jostling taxi drivers all grabbing at your luggage desperate for your fare. And, don't even think of finding a taxi that is even minimally roadworthy. The whole process takes less than an hour.

Some African countries are indeed very efficient. And, thankfully, Brazil no longer requires a visa from us. Something positive has thus fallen.

BLACKFACE, WHITEFACE, ARSE-ABOUT-FACE

March 2015: yet more student pranks were in the news. Further national moral panics centred on cartoons ensued, overshadowing the carnage on the roads, murder, state capture and general social mayhem. All and sundry were writing about the two University of Pretoria drag artists who had clad themselves Al Jolsen-style as maids,[5] and the two Stellenbosch University lads who had dressed up as the Williams tennis sisters.[6]

The link between such daft behaviour was finally being made by press commentators with the kinds of send-ups in which Leon Schuster's candid camera films trade. The difference is that Schuster's films frame their own interpretive contexts. The actual in-the-flesh University of Pretoria residence party at which the foolish two painted their faces black and stuffed the backs of their aprons with large pillows creating big butts lost its context when the images went viral.

Of course, one remembers the University of the Free State Reitz Residence video and the way that the new principal Jonathan Jansen had re-articulated the ensuing damning publicity into a culture change strategy, garnering global support for drawing in an approving Oprah who was awarded an honorary doctorate. In contrast, the University of Pretoria simply used the old *kragdadigheid* (power play) of suspension. Stellenbosch University engaged in re-education activities. Shades of Samora Machel and China? In my old Wits days the most mischief we got up to was when the Knockando Residence guys serenaded the girls' dorms singing radio commercial ditties like 'Ban won't wear off as the day wears long'. The wardens would lock the doors and close the windows lest the girls got the wrong idea.

The issue is that young, techno-savvy, digital natives know what buttons to press, but they usually forget that in pressing buttons they might also *push* a few buttons. Just look at the result. Few thought the Pretoria student skit funny. The extent of its reportage, however, drowned out the Farlam Commission into the shooting by police of 34 real people (miners) at Marikana, not to mention all the other acts of institutional self-destruction, gender-based violence and homicide that undermined our new society every day.

If the University of Pretoria students are rusticated, then what of Schuster? He is the only film director who attracts cross-racial audiences; he was not, until Black Lives Matter in 2020, censured, censored or dragged off to the South African Human Rights Commission. He has been *donnered* (punched) a few times by unwitting angry Afrikaner dupes caught in his often racialised candid camera gags, but then these victims apologise and sign the release form. They can belatedly see the humour in their humiliation and get free tickets to the premier along with Coke and popcorn. But Showmax pulled his films anyway, as their managers suddenly realised that now they actually did not have a sense of humour. Besides, they've made their millions screening his films, sometimes twice or three times a day.

The issue here is not about merits or demerits of students acting stupidly in a country that was facing down a rapidly regressing

Madiba-inspired reconciliation. Neither is it about their actual attitudes, on which no one reported, nor whether or not their drag was 'hate speech', racism or simply farce.

My suggestion was that these students should have asked Schuster to represent them in the subsequent disciplinary hearings. The students might have been persuaded to hang up their costumes or burn them, or place them in Schuster's wardrobe store, or donate them to the Apartheid Museum, founded by the purveyors of carcinogenic skin lighteners, the Krok brothers.[7] If the Kroks can rehabilitate themselves thus, anyone can.

Laughter is how we best deal with our anxieties, prejudices and our own insecurities. Schuster for national psychiatrist or chief sangoma I had suggested. The government is already so over-bloated that one more fat cat in drag milking the taxpayer cows can't do any more krok. He may even do some good, as he has now repented for doing blackface. Psychiatry, psychology or throwing the bones – somebody has to do the dirty work to save South Africans from themselves. Or we could prescribe some Ban deodorant and / or have a national debate about how not to be idiots.

IDIOTS AND ROBOTISATION

Idiotisation enabled by Twitter allows enraged and deranged individuals to dash off stupid remarks ahead of their ability to think judiciously. In the case of opposition MP Diane Kohler-Barnard, she-the-messenger who took the hit for he (a journalist) the twit by sharing a Facebook comment praising apartheid president P.W. Botha.[8] Then there was that expatriate non-entity, Penny, who sparrowed forth on Facebook about blacks being monkeys,[9] dripping dark droppings all over our carefully crafted Zuptanomics-impoverished rainbow nation. Her social media post was pure drivel, but her revealing rabid ravings got more play than any well-composed columnist or farm murders. Sparrow's rantings created a national moral panic, threatening the very fabric of our society, while white monopoly capitalism impoverished the majority. The Human Rights Commission was kept very busy trying to adjudicate on 'hate speech' and when (or if) freedom of speech is subject to censorship. Why do people waste their time responding to such stupid posts when there are far more important issues facing us: refugees on massive scales, wars, terrorism, poverty, environmental destruction, viral pandemics and new pseudo-religions that promote killing, maiming and raping?

Never before in South Africa have so many paintings, sculptures, monuments and buildings, and photographs been defaced, moved, destroyed and hacked, by so many different groups, all at once, some smearing excrement, others imposing their ghastly nakedness upon us in vandalising a photographic exhibition at the University of Cape Town. The Kroks didn't even feature in this national cleansing rite. Even struggle icons were targeted, hammered by the folks so riled up by twitterings about all things that must fall. This kind of stimulus-response behaviour that also typifies social media gives new meaning to the significance of the conditioning of Pavlov's dog to salivate when a bell was rung, which he associated with food. Unthinking salivation, even when bottom-up, is the key to electronic mob rule in the digital age. Economics, sociology, media and psychology textbooks need to be rewritten.

Literary scholars and dramatists have long known satire and the absurd, but irony cannot be encoded in just 140 characters. And these frames of analysis are unacceptable in positivist, hard-nosed science that takes a God's-eye-view of things. But in our world riven with religious conflicts, which, whose and what kind of God are we talking about? Frustratingly, management simply marches on as if managerialism is God. This corporate but blundering God is all-knowing, even as I process master's degree proposals on stakeholder communication, public relations and communication management, all of which argue for bottom-up, rather than top-down management styles. But the gods of these democratic approaches lack presence.

Now, back to fiddling with my smartphone while Rome burns – or is it Zandspruit or Transnet trains, a campus here or there, a few buses, thousands of articulated trucks, secondary schools, municipal buildings and the like?

BEYOND THE ABSURD

The 2016 municipal elections resulted in a hiatus when the Zuptas were accelerating their looting of the economy rather than addressing voter concerns. The absurd and Pythonesque satire had given way to *Mad* magazine's 'Spy vs. Spy'. The 'idiotical' is this magazine's turf. How else could one explain the stand-off between the Treasury, managed by Gordhan and the Gupta surrogates, those nice thieving cabinet ministers who were parodies of themselves? The answer must be in this comic book. The comics (both the authors and the stand-ups) are now the key political jesters and analysts of our age. They have rendered academics and press commentators redundant. The comics, like the e-cow-nomics poster, reach millions. All we can do now is laugh – if anxiously. There is nothing left but stand-up comics like Trevor Noah and cartoonists everywhere.

Comic strip characters are now running for – or are in – office, their hairpieces flapping in the filthy wind generated by their intemperate and undiplomatic speech. Rodrigo Duterte and Donald Trump make Vladimir Putin and Julius Malema seem polite. A bombastic Recep Tayyip Erdoğan switches between hemispheres and Turkish academics, teachers, judges have been arrested in the tens of thousands. Kim Jong-un's fireworks rattle everyone: 'Making the world a deadlier place', crooned *Mad*. These clowns replaced other nutters like Silvio Berlusconi and then Zuma who thought that government was a 24/7 sex party. Brazil's Jair Bolsonaro is happy for the Amazon rainforests to burn, for COVID-19 to kill hundreds of thousands, and he could not care less about the indigenous losing their territory to louts, loggers and landgrabbers. And let's not forget all those forgettable Australian prime ministers who regularly and viciously depose each other through a revolving door, even as Australia burns to oblivion and climate change denial continues. Saddam Hussein would routinely fire weapons in public and Mad Bob up north fired 25 000 (un)civil servants in 2016 because there was no money left to pay for no service.

The world is 'flush with comedy' and 'You will want to sit down for this', says *Mad*. Well, the Cape Town pooh brigade not only sat down, but picked it up, democratically spreading their excrement over statues, steps and places they did not like. Even Schuster had not shrunk to these depths, though *Mr Bones* came quite close. No wonder the *Mr Bones* trilogy blockbustered the box office. During apartheid, Afrikaans-language films were replete with images of lavatories as metaphorical indicators of their directors 'up yours' attitude to authority, censorship and oppressive ideology. But (the fired) Hlaudi Motsoening (CEO of the South African Broadcasting Corporation) could not find censorship anywhere even as he and his goons imposed it everywhere. *Mad* magazine's 'Weird Al' is the scourge of the crackpots and the dumbest everywhere. Spies, spoofery, spooks – they are so busy taking each other out that they forget about what is good for the nation. Make a comic character the president.

As the popular American film critic Roger Ebert puts it: 'I plundered it [*Mad*] for clues to the universe.'[10] Sadly, *Mad* fell in 2019 after 67 years of cartooning, but like the *Starship Enterprise*'s search for the final frontier, *Mad* will continue in books and special collections – thankfully. The spooks will still be pilloried.

Notes

1. See https://brandanreynolds.com

2. The showerhead affixed to Zuma's skull in cartoons drawn by Zapiro (Jonathan Shapiro) began when he testified in his 2006 rape trial that he had had unprotected sex with a young woman whom he knew to be HIV positive. To protect himself from contracting HIV himself, he said, he had showered afterwards

3. Read more at: http://www.iol.co.za/dailynews/news/matric-art-pupils-satirical-t-shirts-infuriate-kzn-anc-1602795

4. Read more at: https://www.iol.co.za/business-report/economy/laugh-it-off-can-now-guffaw-after-ruling-752051

5. Read more at: http://mg.co.za/article/2014-08-09-blackface-students-suspended-from-residences

6. Read more at: http://www.iol.co.za/news/south-africa/western-cape/blackface-scandal-hits-stellenbosch-1755477

7. Read more at: http://mg.co.za/article/2006-05-02-lighter-is-fairer. The Kroks tried after the end of apartheid to sanitise their unsavory reputations by establishing the Apartheid Museum. See also https://www.popmatters.com/sassen020501-2496174194.html

8. Read more at: http://www.news24.com/SouthAfrica/News/Little-sympathy-for-Kohler-Barnard-after-PW-post-20151002

9. Read more at: http://mg.co.za/article/2016-01-04-twitter-erupts-after-kzn-estate-agent-calls-black-people-monkeys

10. Read more at: http://www.rogerebert.com/rogers-journal/introduction-mad-about-the-movies

10 *Culture Can Kill*

Abortion, penis enlargement and all manner of pseudo-medical treatments and psychological services are visible in newspaper classified adverts, street trash bins, tree trunks and telephone poles, all over South Africa.[1] Muti, magic and mystery can be dispensed by consulting this shaman or that *inyanga* or someone calling himself 'doctor' or a call to a no-name cell phone number. Failing romantic relationships can be fixed and advice on how to win the Lottery is legion.

Such advertising and chicanery is commonplace. Other than the odd academic (De Lange 2015, 2017) and some who claim that this sector is of cultural significance, no one complains, no one is dragged before the Advertising Standards Authority and few are held to account for botched procedures. The public health sector picks up the tab. The tatty posters remain in place and neither the advertisers nor the printers are charged with publishing false medical promises. However, it must be added that it was a criminal offence to circulate 'fake' claims about COVID-19, whether on how the virus spreads or on claimed cures, during the 2020 South African state of disaster.

Between 2015 and 2017, one globally known University of Cape Town medico, Professor Tim Noakes, was pilloried, exposed and reduced to tears in front of a Health Professions Council inquiry for offering supposedly 'harmful' nutritional advice on Twitter to a new mom. Why? Because he publicly identified all the junk we were told as kids is 'good for you' (sugar, preservatives, low fat and salt, especially). Like thousands of other diet pushers, he experimented on himself, but he also scientifically analysed the results and popularised the Banting approach, which took on the obesity, cardiac and carcinogenic industries. The Heart Foundation got into a tizz, the sugar industry went into fizzy spin and the medical fraternity fried him in a hearing.

Yet *Noseweek, Carte Blanche* and individual journalists continuously expose certified doctors who kill, maim and disfigure, often with impunity. Maybe these charlatans also advertise on street poles. They have protective magic, those poles. And what does the academic establishment do in cases of self-experimentation? Complain about the lack of control groups and transgression of ethical clearance procedures. How does one apply for ethical clearance to experiment on oneself? Is that ethical? Autoethnographers do it all the time. Moreover, just ask the directors of our medical aids which diet they use – Banting will probably feature prominently.

So, what is going on here? Entrenched interests? Targeted victimisation? Sham science? Consultations cannot be offered through social media, proclaimed one psychiatrist, they must be referred to a medical practitioner. He or she may have never have heard of the University of the Witwatersrand's (Wits) Dr Harry Seftel who, with the South African Broadcasting Corporation's (SABC) radio doctor, dispensed good sense weekly over the airwaves during the 1980s. Perhaps this psycho should try to find a doctor in a rural area, an informal settlement or even in a formal one?

Renegade physicist Derek Wang used to tell our honours students from both the humanities and science when he taught Science as a Cultural Expression to 'beware of actors wearing white coats pretending to be doctors in TV ads'. Adverts use rhetorical proofs and create an impression of evidence. Wang discussed causality and belief when he threw the bones while teaching and he prescribed the *I Ching*, an ancient Chinese divination text. *The Doctors* television programme has turned healthcare into an entertaining talk show and television dramas like *ER* depict surgical procedures wrongly about half the time. Just shows, one cannot trust actors/doctors wearing white coats – they can kill.

Some smokers I know have been persuaded by tobacco companies that smoking is not unhealthy. Indeed, the smell of third-hand smoke lingered in the waiting room of a physician specialist I was required to consult by my insurance company. Not a good advert for the medico or the insurer! How can I trust a wheezing specialist whose white coat reeked of smoke while he was fitting me up on his ECG? When working with a global public health communication project I was astonished that so many eminent non-governmental organisation workers, who were advising the masses on health and life skills, were themselves inveterate smokers.

The magical health myths extend to the marijuana lobby, masked under the acronym, CBD. Purveyors of death and ill-health include car manufacturers, the junk food and fizzy drink industries and alcohol producers who aim their adverts at teeny boppers. The list is endless. And very few watchdogs target the self-styled nutritionists who persuade with their before-and-after doctored photographs. Indeed, one charlatan took on the Advertising Standards Authority and won simply because the manufacturer did not subscribe to the Authority's code of conduct.

Yet the majority of South Africans are hungry, nutritionally lacking and unhealthy, no matter how much they are eating. But the obsessives focused on Noakes and forgot the bigger picture. Humiliate him, but then get your penis enlarged from a quack who only has a cell phone number attached to a pavement rubbish bin. I am all for taking medical care onto the streets and not just Harley Street or Lancet Hall.

Visit any pharmaceutical chain store. The queue winds purchasers cheek-by-jowl alongside child-accessible shelves displaying junk food, chewable rubbish and sweets. Health warnings are not required. This junk undoes the good that the medicine fixes that they actually came to the store to buy. Once hospitals actually contributed to their own profits by permitting smoking and providing cigarette-dispensing machines. Yet, during the pandemic lockdowns, one could buy sweets but not books. Something went wrong.

We are our own worst enemies. We are complicit with the charlatans in the shopping malls and God knows who the nutters are who rely on the street pole dispensers.

CULTURE AND INITIATION

Post-puberty black men are sent to slaughter in the name of culture. Thus argued *Sunday Times* columnist Barney Mthombothi (2019), alongside two letters questioning the president of the Congress of Traditional Leaders of South Africa, Mathupa Mokoena, and his 'we've always done it this way' dogma. An adjacent editorial, 'We Need to Care More', referred to the deaths of young men in the Eastern Cape annual circumcision ritual. A third letter, 'A Better Way to Treat Beale', lamented the humiliating way that the doctor, some of whose recent patients had died during operations, had been arrested. He fled into hiding in September 2020 when his co-accused, anaesthetist Dr Abdulhay Munshi, was seemingly assassinated in the street.

Over 500 young boys died at initiation schools between 2015 and 2019. Less than 75 cases were brought to court, with only 14 convictions. The sham reasoning that justifies these different situations is akin to AIDS denialism, rejection of science and the assumption that 'culture' is God.

I prefer Mthombothi's definition: however defined, culture 'tends to create walls and trenches'. Dr Beale, working under controlled, observable conditions, was arrested, while rogue and approved Eastern Cape initiation schools get a free pass to mutilate and kill en masse – in the name of Culture/God and 'tradition'. 'Culture' is simply a way of making sense, one among many. The Congress of Traditional Leaders assumes that culture is immutably fixed and not subject to change. In fact, culture is constantly altering.

Multiple medical systems coexist in South Africa: first is the regulated, legally accountable one in which doctors Beale and Munshi worked. Second, a parallel sector consists of sangomas (indigenous healers) and *izinyanga* (herbalists) trained via apprenticeship, whom the majority consult. Then, third, there are butchers who operate from the unregulated, anonymous street-based informal sector that advertises via street pamphlets. This is the sector in which the illegal and even some legal initiation schools' surgeries are located.

But these instances pale when it comes to 'voodoo economics', a term reportedly coined by a temporarily disorientated cabinet minister when he allegedly fell for the Mbeki-era garlic and olive oil theory of HIV cures during the era of denialism, which resulted in the premature deaths of 350 000 South Africans, a Harvard University study revealed, justified by sham science published in dodgy journals that scientists themselves had rejected. During the COVID-19 pandemic, Indonesia advocated bean sprouts, broccoli and prayer and rejected as insulting a Harvard University report on its denialism. The Indian prime minister, Narendra Modi, was telling Indians to clap, bang on utensils and light lamps to address the situation while doctors and nurses were being beaten up or threatened because they did not have the cure (Satish Kolluri, Association for Cultural Studies circular, 3 April 2020). President Trump in the United States endorsed the populist raving that COVID-19 was an attempted Democratic Party coup-by-panic, which represented the Mark of the Beast, the anti-Christ. He proposed injecting detergent as a cure and when this manuscript went to print, well over 250 000 Americans had died of the virus. Madagascar's President Andry Rajoelina launched a herbal remedy called Covid-Organics that he claimed would act both as a cure and a vaccine, sharing images of the bottled fluid on his social media page.

A national media, educational and health HIV and AIDS campaign was implemented by the Department of Health between

1996 and 2000. But the minister's advisory committee, on which I served and which devised the strategy, was constantly distracted by having to extinguish fires ignited from her office: Virodene, *Sarafina II*, illegal experimentation on unwitting subjects, vegetable cures and, inevitably, 'culture'. South Africa's health services were totally derailed – as was the new nation. Little did we know that this was just the start of the fake cure industry that was to become a global curse in 2020.

The formal medical sector and taxpayer have to deal with the consequences caused by sham science that overpowers good sense. Ideology is the semantic scaffolding that shapes interpretations, it tells us what to think, while culture accounts for the content of what people think and do. Science explores inherited ways of making sense and then proposes solutions. Properly done, a caring science transgresses ideological and cultural walls and escapes trenches, as occurred with the end of denialism. New and better ways of doing things emerge, though Trump re-legitimated sham reasoning with regard to COVID-19, even as his country paid a terrible price for this denialism.

The denial of regressive aspects of culture is the same discourse that casts a blind eye over the systematic assassination of 200+, mostly foreign, truck drivers on South African national highways during 2018/19. Thousands of their vehicles were torched because 'our culture' cannot tolerate foreigners or alien cultures. Few perpetrators were held to account. Xenophobia is linked to this frame of myopic reference and entrenched positions refuse to see the light.

The answers are simple. But they are clouded by ideology and South Africans more often than not pursue the most complicated and self-destructive ways of resolving social problems. The formal health sector, for example, can (and sometimes does) collaborate with traditional medicine practitioners, local clinics with the *abakwetta* (Xhosa initiates), hygienically and safely fusing the traditions of pre-modernity and modernity, the past with the present, and culture with caring. Like legacy surgical instruments, modern ones also need to be clean, and aftercare a prerequisite – enforced dehydration for cultural purposes cannot be appropriate.

A colleague from the Eastern Cape explained the depth of the cultural contradictions:

> A neighbour of mine lost their grandson to initiation. The father's brother is a doctor who would dutifully watch over him. The boy developed a urinary infection due to probably unhygienic practices. He refused water and food, dehydrated and died within 10 days of the circumcision. To cover up the initiation school set his hut alight and claimed they had all gone into town to a bar and on return found his hut burnt down with his remains in it. I asked his grandparents several times about the SAPS's [South African Police Service's] and forensic investigation, with no reply. The adults involved are in the first instance a retired school teacher and a qualified nursing sister. In the second case the mother is a psychologist. ALL well educated people. The women say that initiation is in the male domain and the men say it is culture. Chiefs, are responsible for initiation schools, but a money buys silence and abuses culture. Girls are used to lure boys to the bush as they get ridiculed by the girls for not being circumcised. The problems are twofold: the first is corruption/money and the second is this dogmatic approach to the past practices instead of allowing the practice to develop with the times. The real problem does not lie with the above but with the reinforced belief transmitted to the young boys/men that once you have achieved manhood you as a male are more important than a woman and that she as the lesser person is subservient to you. AND SO WE CRY ABOUT THE RAPE, MURDER, ABUSE AND GENERAL DISREGARD

SHOWN TO WOMEN. I ask, how much bigger is the problem than what gets into the press? I believe culture is like LPG. It is inert until a human hand meddles with it. Stop worrying about the tools of identity and concern yourself with the hands that misuse or represent the tools. (Roger Carter, email, 5 January 2020)

Along with Carter and Mthombothi, I agree that we need to get out of the cultural trenches, we have to escape the tyranny of patriarchy as narrated in the timely 2017 film *The Wound* (directed by John Trengrove). This transgressive story offers insight on an urban boy's traditional initiation ritual and the secret homosexuality of his mentors in an Eastern Cape mountain retreat. The film and its makers became the target of the fixed, fuming fascist and homophobic cultural commissars, who alleged the wounding of their patriarchal ethnic pride. Accused of cultural insensitivity, in fact, the film frames the issue differently as a negotiation between pre-modernity and postmodernity, even as its actors had to go into hiding after the film's release and the title was pulled from most cinemas.

Caring is key. Speaking out is crucial. Doing something is necessary: better regulation, accountability and enforcement of safety mechanisms where the unregulated health sectors are concerned. Culture will take care of itself but it must be critically debated. It is not immutably fixed in time, content or belief. Just as initiation schools should be regulated, so should wet markets where living and dead exotic wild animals are held in insanitary cages alongside domesticated fauna and sold for human consumption. Thankfully, one outcome of COVID-19 saw dogs reclassified from livestock to pets (or companion animals) in China.

Such cultural practices should nurture rather than kill. Animals are part of culture. They can catalyse social interactions, healing and community. Just visit any dog park where their humans think of them as people, rather than brutalising them through lack of care and attention; bored barking dogs as just another backup to one's armed response home alarm system. The ontological distinction between humans and non-humans is being increasingly questioned in what is called critical animal studies, from anthropology to organisational sciences. A social justice perspective on human-animal relations tries to contribute to an intellectual argument to take non-human animals more seriously as co-citizens in the (organisational) life world. This may have wide-ranging implications for our lifestyles, ranging from the types of food we eat to the liquids we drink and the ways we think about our claimed human superiority in this world, says Harry Wels (2013). COVID-19 and so many other viruses that kill humans occur because our behaviour neglects an awareness of animal rights and their ecological functions.

Did we have to wait for French deconstructionst Jaques Derrida (2008) to confirm ethnological science that most – if not all – European philosophy has been biased and speciesist in assuming the positivist distinction between human and animal? Human and non-human animals can only be distinguished from each other in degree, but not in kind. Remember the *Homo naledi* furore, which angered prominent politicos who misunderstand evolution and who refused to decentre humans in the broader scheme of things? Is this rejection not another form of othering, of apartheid, based on species rather than race? A new inclusive paradigm is, however, emerging, which will hopefully enable us to manage flu viruses as a problem of culture and not just a biomedical one (see Chapter 11).

The often destructive relationships with non-human animals could not be more urgent in the light of current global debates concerning the increasing rapidity of what is known as the sixth mass extinction, which started with the spread of humankind 80 000 years go and reached a tipping point in 2016. Natural causes are not the sole explanation for species extinction this time. Solutions that address the natural deficit by working with the 'species turn' by anthropology and organisational studies, especially, is long overdue. As the planet faces catastrophe, new paradigms are emerging, but can they gain legitimacy quickly enough by scientists and especially politicians and consumers to make a difference? These include the proposal that it may be fruitful to treat non-human animals as actual agentic stakeholders in research and analysis. How does one request consent from animals if one is not a qualified whisperer?

How would our pets (or wild animals) qualify us? Now, there is a conundrum. Just read Lawrence Anthony's (2009) or Ian Player's (1998) books for a new paradigm. The problem is there are no university courses in 'whispering', so only those in the know know. But there is hope. Horses are now being used by their whisperers to teach management communication.[2] All the while horses continue to be mistreated well into what appears to be the closing period of the Enlightenment.[3]

While the bodies of knowledge and associated bodies of practice relating to multi-species ethnographies are relatively new in the Western academic enterprise, they have a long history among indigenous people, who relied on their knowledge of the environment and fauna and flora, the seasons, climate and astronomy for their survival and livelihoods. But positivist science delayed the development of this intuitive knowledge in the industrial academy, to the detriment of non-human species and the environment in general. Even so, once hunting and gathering communities adopted rifle technology, the environment (and they) often paid the inevitable price.

Is there a reason why 'pet' and 'pest' are so similar in their spelling? Are we humans not the pests? After all, we have destroyed nearly all the original habitats of undomesticated animals and shot, sold and branded most of the rest. We have denied animals consciousness-awareness-just-like-us, what Wels (2013) calls 'whispering empathy', as Stephen Hawking and others have also acknowledged.[4] Old habits die hard and quackery remains a predominant discourse of the day.

QUACKERY AND PSEUDOSCIENCE

Given Thabo Mbeki's AIDS denialism, it is very fitting that South
Africa hosted the first International Summit on Quackery and
Pseudoscience in 2017. It was organised by George Claassen, director
of the Centre for Science and Technology at Stellenbosch University.
The delegates examined the role of science communication in the
medical arena in countering quackery. Quackery means a hawker
of salve, not the two-legged amphibian, whom I will now use in a
metaphorical sense.

Traditional medicine has its place. This I learned in the mid-1970s
when making a film for a Wits psychology professor on *twasas*, or
trainee sangomas. During student fieldtrips in 2017/18 into the
bush we met, talked to and hoped to hear the ancestors speaking
through the mystical (real) white lions, who have a particular place
in Venda mythology (Tucker 2016). Extraordinary things are said to
happen on the African Ivory Route, none of them, the guides claim,
being scientifically explainable. Communicating with lions (or
elephants or horses) requires an affective science whereas talking
to quacks requires the suspension of science or replacement with
pseudoscience and sham reasoning.

Claassen, a veteran science journalist, is a man whose ditty duck-
tape discourse is after my own heart. He turned the tables on the
quackers who proposed this toxic brew as a cure for AIDS and the
African National Congress's (ANC) ballooning party debt. And
what a party that was. Just ask anyone who was working in the
health sector in the late 1990s. When cooperating with the harassed,
hardworking and sensible officials in the Department of Health,
we all tried to restore sanity to the upper duckhouse (Cabinet).
The politicos touting 'traditional' treatments could not care less
about treatments and cures; they just want to be 'seen' to be doing
something, while doing nothing. The Life Esidimeni debacle (2015–
17), and the refusal of the provincial executive council member to

take responsibility or even understand her complicity, arises out of this culture of narcissism and impunity, lack of accountability and blatant idiocy. The Ombudsman, Professor W.M. Makgoba, exposed this sham project that led to the estimated 156 unnecessary deaths of physically and mentally challenged patients, often in the most appalling of circumstances. The consequences of this lack of accountability dwarfs the callousness of the police massacre at Marikana of 34 miners.

On the AIDS issue, eventually, the light of day reappeared; denialism, sham reasoning and quackery retreated and the health sector was able deliver drugs for HIV again. Finally, academics are now taking on the quacks and explaining why they have such wide purchase across all societies. The quacks were very quickly outlawed by President Cyril Ramaphosa's state of disaster proclamation on COVID-19 during early 2020 and many of the scientific members of the former minister's HIV and AIDS advisory committee, discarded by the Cabinet a decade earlier, reappeared in full force. They were this time given all the resources and media exposure they needed to do their jobs without state hindrance. Science trumped sham reasoning in this instance in South Africa at least.

While we at universities critique the cultural commissars, what about our own institutions?

SAFE SPACES

Our economy might be in the doldrums, but if exporting protest and infrastructural vandalism could be commoditised we would be in the pound seats. #RhodesMustFall reached as far away as Oxford University. No sooner had the pooh dried on Rhodes' statue at the University of Cape Town than American students started demanding 'safe spaces' on campuses and an end to 'institutional violence', 'micro-aggressions' and 'trigger' words, comments or phrases and, crucially, sexual assault.

These students won some concessions, including the establishment of a 'Department of Inclusion' at the University of Missouri, where administrators are now obliged to undergo 'implicit bias training, which, though incurable, can be minimised'.[5] The 'Safe Space' provided by Brown University includes a room 'equipped with cookies, colouring-in books, bubbles, Play-Doh, calming music, pillows, blankets and a video of frolicking puppies, as well as students and staff members trained to deal with trauma'.[6]

Such campus threats pale into insignificance compared to the mass murders on American streets, on their campuses, from primary schools to universities, nightclubs, places of worship, workplaces and parks. Even during the COVID-19 lockdown, American citizens in some states could buy guns, deemed an essential service, but not books. And while the United States battles its own psychological demons, back home an SABC audience during 2016 would have been spared witnessing the televised horror of protest violence on the streets, thanks to SABC's Hlaudi '90 per cent local content' Motsoeneng. Frankly, if any place merits being a designated a 'safe space', it is our own homes. We therefore need to be more appreciative of Motsoeneng's heroic but failed effort to deliver 'safe space television' and radio that does not hurt anyone's feelings that will allow us to float more gently into slumber not vexed with distressing nightmares and the staggering numbers of COVID-19 infections and associated deaths.

We are not alone in this noble quest. England is now a 'safe space' from European refugees and immigrants by Brexiting. Trump tried to create a 'safe space' from South Americans by building a Great Wall of America and the banning of immigrants from some Muslim countries, but his lethargy could not create a safe space from COVID-19, so he also blamed the World Health Organisation for his failure. Anywhere outside of Zimbabwe is a 'safer space' for Zimbabweans. And national borders were reinstated by the European Union during the epidemic.

While I am receiving long-overdue treatment for the implicit bias and micro/macro-aggression in my writing, the challenges facing academics are actually life threatening.

STRESS, ILLNESS AND EARLY RETIREMENT

Academic work has a rapidly increasing half-life while the half-life of academics is becoming a serious problem. Unless this is arrested, there will be few of us left.

But the madness – what I diagnose as academentia – continues.

Globally, academics are wilting under stress – 60–80-hour working weeks – and not surprisingly, dying prematurely, falling ill and taking early retirement, with B&Bs having, until COVID-19, been the preferred option for continuing income generation. Just doing one's job has become life threatening. A dean of education, for example, was assassinated at the University of Zululand, allegedly for exposing a campus-based syndicate issuing fraudulent PhDs,[7] while some vice-chancellors and deans periodically require bodyguards to protect them from vandals within the gates.

Campus massacres are common in the United States. For example, on 12 February 2010, an assistant professor at the University of Alabama shot six colleagues at a routine departmental meeting. 'Anonymous Academic', published in *The Guardian* in March 2014, describes the funeral of 'J', a British PhD student who committed suicide. The writer wondered if the stress of doctoral work had caused his colleague's suicide, attracting a massive response.[8]

We all know colleagues who have died too young. We all know that academia actually does make one ill. Just ask any health service provider. Does anyone listen? Academics, administrators and support staff always commented (reflectively) on my columns, management hardly ever! The result: academics from a variety of disciplines increasingly are resorting to satire to characterise academentia, which is now a global pandemic.[9]

A cure must be found.

Notes

1. Read more at: http://www.news24.com/SouthAfrica/Local/Hillcrest-Fever/Illegal-abortion-posters-litter-streets-20150824-25

2. Read more at: http://www.festo-didactic.co.uk/gb-en/open-courses/all-open-courses-dates/people/management/horse-whispering-leadership-lessons-in-coaching.htm

3. See Avaaz, 'Stop the Pregnant Horse Trade', https://secure.avaaz.org/campaign/en/horse_blood_loc/?tOJDIab&v=500274238&cl=11597066168&_checksum=8a9a26b14375df54d6bb5e0709cb2c896cc258924ecfedeff7e6104826

4. Read more on the Cambridge Declaration on Consciousness in Non-Human Animals at: http://io9.com/5937356/

5. Read more at: http://libraryguides.missouri.edu/c.php?g=557234&p=3832208

6. Read more at: http://www.nytimes.com/2015/03/22/opinion/sunday/judith-shulevitz-hiding-from-scary-ideas.html

7. See https://citizen.co.za/news/south-africa/2044785/professor-at-unizulu-murdered-for-uncovering-syndicate-of-fraudulent-phds/

8. See https://www.theguardian.com/higher-education-network/blog/2014/mar/01/mental-health-issue-phd-research-university

9. Read more at: http://www.politicsweb.co.za/opinion/sas-demoralized-academic-staff; http://www.scottishreview.net/JillStephenson118.shtml; http://www.theguardian.com/higher-education-network/2014/mar/06/mental-health-academics-growing-problem-pressure-university?CMP=fb_gu; http://www.educationviews.org/dark-thoughts-mental-illness-rise-academia/; see also 'The Travelling Supervisor', *The Witness*, 8 June 2018

11 *The Academentia Sunrise*

The narrative developed in this book might be considered somewhat pessimistic, so I will conclude on a more optimistic note by offering a Happiness Index for universities, and then develop the skeleton for a theory of 'gotchacology', where academics not only checkmate, but also constructively engage with managerialism.

Happiness is when Keynesian economics replaces neoliberalism and all those utterly reductive and anti-humanist e-cow-nomics approaches discussed in earlier chapters. John Maynard Keynes's theory (1936) addressed the traumas of the Great Depression and critiqued classical economic arguments that natural economic forces and incentives would be sufficient for economic recovery. This was the lesson learned from COVID-19 when governments enacted massive stimulus packages and social support mechanisms to mitigate the economic and social effects of the pandemic, though in South Africa, needless to say, race-based black economic empowerment (BEE) criteria continued to bedevil allocations, excluding foreign nationals and so-called whites even though the virus itself does not discriminate on the basis of race, nationality, gender or class.[1] But, needless to say, corruption again loomed large when the media revealed the unbelievable extent of the pillage by the newly styled Covid-preneurs who not only stole from the state, but also provided substandard products that probably did kill some patients. Cyril Ramaphosa, the post-Zupta, conspicuously honest president hung his head in shame on national television.

For universities, happiness, specifically, occurs when:

- purchase orders are dealt with correctly and timeously;
- payroll has not forgotten to pay staff and post-doctoral fellows;

- deans can again be academic leaders;
- budgets are allocated on time;
- classrooms are made into welcoming, enabling, interactive, noise-free pedagogical spaces where students want to be;
- public spaces are properly maintained and students learn to respect them *and* the cleaners who clean up after them;
- management realises that their job is to ensure a fully functioning institution-wide operational environment, to enable academics to do their jobs properly and to help us meet our so-called productivity units;
- universities remember that they are learning organisations, not factories that manufacture graduates on a production line and demand articles for rent-seeking purposes;
- collegiality is restored by simple things like well-appointed staff tearooms, emitting the aroma of good, affordable coffee, where newspapers can be read and where we can all relax and talk for a few moments without having to tick a leave form;
- top management is seen to be consorting collegially with the plebs, experiencing life at the eduface, the student-face and the coalface;
- all staff treat each other with respect, forging a common project;
- staff (who are humans too) are considered as ends in themselves, and not as a means to someone else's ends, and when Human Resources actually comes to realise this – otherwise 'human resources' is a contradiction in terms;
- stress levels are creatively managed by the institution to lessen the burnout factor and increased costs to medical aids;
- students complain rather than cheer when a class is cancelled;

- students come to class to study rather than just to do time and sign a register or to enforce closure of the campus, and sometimes to burn it;
- students come to class prepared, rather than waiting passively to be taught;
- lecturers enable students' self-learning, rather than creating dependency;
- students respect lecturer's privacy, space and time;
- leave categories are reconfigured to enable academics to get out of their offices and to teach from the field in the real world; and
- students spend their National Student Financial Aid Scheme bursaries on books rather than alcohol and airtime.

If we can implement the 'whens', we can stop being 'when-we's' and join in the larger future-oriented project. Let us get beyond Jones's Law, as applied by Donald Trump in demonising China (as in the 'Chinese virus') and the World Health Organisation, which states: 'The man who can smile when things go wrong has thought of someone he can blame them on' (Martin 1973:25).

RETIREMENT AND GOTCHACOLOGY

As will have become clear, one of the benefits of science is the law-making process. Scientists have laws and principles for everything: Boyle's Law, the Law of Averages, the Heisenberg Uncertainly Principle, and so on. These laws and principles account for the behaviour of chemical, physical and measurable phenomena. Many business laws as discussed by T.L. Martin (1973) explain irrationality while others identify why organisations that claim to be efficient and that institute endless performance management exercises, departmental assessments and never-ending audits are, in fact, so chaotic. My study of academentia pays homage to all these laws and describes the experiences of the subjects of these laws.

In 2013, I was hosted by an Australian university. This was a truly liminal experience – that is, a quality of ambiguity or disorientation occurred during a ritual, in this case a retirement event. An internationally influential cultural studies professor, Graeme Turner, a critic of neoliberalism and institutional stupidity, was retiring. Not only was an entire afternoon devoted to discussions and critique of his life's work, its impacts and its significance for Australians, but a celebratory evening rounded off the day's events.

In South Africa, retirees slink away in the dark of night, often to a deafening institutional silence. At the University of Queensland, luminaries came in from all over the world to debate, celebrate and pay homage. The seminar symbolised both tangible and intangible academic value, rather than only crude, quantifiable, tick-box productivity units. The deliberations highlighted the critical cuts of academic integrity rather than sycophantic posturing.

The cocktail party after the seminar offered an eye-opening performance in academic politics. The *acting* vice-chancellor got a huge cheer when she stepped up to the podium; the *acting* deputy vice-chancellor (Research) was noisily applauded when he followed and the *acting* dean was met with a thundering ovation when he was introduced. The reverse signifier, of course, related to the *absence* (because they were all on suspension) of the previous (permanent) People of Worth (PoW), the incumbents of these high management positions. Academocracy does still somehow exist in some institutions, in some places, some of the time. Liminality – the case here – enables the reversal or temporary suspension of hierarchies, while taken-for-granted future outcomes are cast into doubt.

The discussions were grounded on Turner's extensive influence on national policy and global debate. His often mentioned 'F*ck that' attitude towards despotism, regression and institutional and individual idiocy became the metaphor that was often mentioned in jest by his peers, but uttered with deadly theoretical intent. He put it more subtly when, in defeating counter-democratic tendencies in academic decision-making, he simply said 'Gotcha!'

The gotcha factor is what increasingly comes to mind as everything unravels around us, even as more and more performance management systems are put in place, and more and more rules are enacted in every institution everywhere. As John Collier put it:

> I find this whole performance management process unedifying and rather insulting. A nasty corporate American import which in reality only serves to undermine people's loyalty in an institution, panders to victimisation and the creation of unnecessary enmities, and promotes, not excellency, but mediocrity – the last being the greatest scourge our university faces, and which we must fight against where possible. However, performance management is here and here to stay, so we must bite the bullet.

Stress wrought by autocracy is shovelled downwards and academic workers everywhere have been restricted from the previously safe spaces like Council, Senate and faculty boards, in which they can play the Gotcha game. But they are not yet fully counter-Gotcha-ed. Consider this response to my columns from someone in a support division from an electrical engineering department: 'Your ability to capture the feelings of both staff and students is almost supernatural. Your courage to put them in words gives me optimism and hope that things will improve. I am sure that the change starts with us rather than the fear of what might be done to us.'

This comment encodes exactly what my colleague from Australia stands for. Turner's new playing field was the national one, one on which he intended to play Gotcha on a much larger scale. In the South African context, Jonathan Jansen is one of the few who works in the national 'F*ck that ....' liminal space.

The University of KwaZulu-Natal once had its own Gotcha exponent. This was the irrepressible, hugely articulate, really fearsome, thundering mathematics professor, John Swart. He was the only member of Senate who could stare down vice-chancellors – *any* vice-chancellors. He always took an opposing view to force the linear thinkers to think dialectically when trying to make policy that actually worked in the implementation. He required Senate to think, to debate and to act with integrity, and to consider and weigh up the consequences of its decisions. He needed to, for as veteran staff member Mohamed Haffajee observed:

> I too came here ages ago, in 1984, in fact, and I have survived, nay crawled, through battlefields worse than the Somme, mustard gas and pummeled from bureaucracies afar, and lived. I've seen eight – at the last count – VCs [vice-chancellors] come and go and leave with a 'newer, better' system for us, from the erstwhile UDW [University of Durban–Westville] to the now highly successful (417th best university in the world, is it?) UKZN [University of KwaZulu-Natal], and survived, like you and many other unsung battle-hardened soldiers. Treblinka, Lubyanka, we've done them all.
> Or should I say, we've outlasted them all! And just when you thought that it was safe to get back in the water…, there's a new fresh VC at the gate.

Hierarchiology explains why there are so few John Swarts in top management anywhere now in the world of academentia. Gresham's Law explains that 'trivial matters are handled promptly', with the corollary that 'important matters are never solved' (cited in Martin 1973: 81). This law, operative in committology corresponds with a chemistry law, the Berthelot Principle: 'Of all possible reactions, the one that does occur will liberate the greatest amount of heat'.

Translated into academentia, heat means 'hot air', that is, there is nothing to be done but we can talk lots about it. Committees and meetings simply recirculate the heat and the meeting becomes more important than does the problem the meeting was constituted to solve. This is Hendrickson's Law, derived from environmental engineering.

The Turner retirement seminar was not hot air. It achieved something. It placed human value on a human being by his fellow humans. While some human resource boxes might have been ticked, the symbolic quality of this send-off could not be quantified.

I used to be an occasional Gotcha man at UKZN. My last dean there told me that in the institutional scheme of things I was considered a 'trouble maker' – but the go-to man when utter upper-management stupidity needed to be corrected. I thank the man from Australia for enabling this new theory in gotchacology.

COVID-19 AS GOTCHA

When visiting Beijing, I always remarked on my eerie experience of not hearing or seeing birds, or seeing the sun, masked as it was behind shiny, thin shards of angular white light refracted by pervasive brown airborne pollution that blanketed thousands of square kilometres. My Chinese colleagues usually were unperturbed, as environmental health was only just coming onto the national agenda following the 2008 Olympics when clean air was a precondition of being awarded the contract.

The ecological correction precipitated by the COVID-19 virus, however, resulted in an unparalleled global effort to flatten the curve of spatial infection, giving governments time to prepare their health systems and social containment strategies as the virus spread from China across the world. Animal trafficking, the systematic mistreatment of wild and domesticated animals and fish, creates conditions for the periodic emergence of viral cultures in street wet markets and other congested and insanitary public spaces. These viruses then travel along human transport routes. Such viruses are sourced partly to ideologically fixed regressive conceptions of culture – 'we've always done it like this' – and a refusal to address the health, social and environmental consequences. As Sonja Shah observes:

> For decades, we've sated our outsized appetites by encroaching on an ever-expanding swath of the planet with our industrial activities, forcing wild species to cram into remaining fragments of habitat in closer proximity to ours. That's what has allowed animal microbes such as SARS-COV2 – not to mention hundreds of others from Ebola to Zika – to cross over into human bodies, causing epidemics. In theory, we could decide to shrink our industrial footprint and conserve wildlife habitat, so that animal microbes stay in animals' bodies, instead. (Shah 2020)

Given the entitlement pressures legitimised by unfettered consumption, this is unlikely, Shah avers, in which case, mandatory paid sick leave will move from the margins to the centre of policy debates. Restrictions on intimacy will see the end of the hype around online education, as a generation forced into seclusion will reshape the culture around a contrarian appreciation for unsanitary communal life. Already this was happening after the 2020 lockdowns in the guise of Trumpian rallies, biker rallies, beach-going and other superspreader events.

Chapter 10 offers some examples with regard to HIV and AIDS, traditional initiation, sham medical street hawkers and the traditionalist obsession with imagined past practices that imprison whole societies within self-destructive behavioural practices. Allied to these killer discourses and their associated medical conditions have been the dodgy researchers and the journals that legitimised denialism, and who found beguiling official support from reigning presidents in South Africa during the HIV/AIDS epidemic during the early 2000s; and then in the United States in early 2020, when Trump, in his usual racist diatribe, described COVID-19 as a 'Chinese virus'. This was a virulent politics playing on nativist fear and causing moral panics against migrants, refugees, Asians and others, like Democrats, and even Corona Beer, brewed in Mexico. The virus was associated with the way people look, a kind of false association that underpins the whole reductionist philosophy of racial classification as it is applied in South Africa (see Saunderson-Meyer 2020).

Even in China, politics delayed a medical response – the doctor who blew the whistle on COVID-19 was arrested and made to recant for allegedly causing social despondency. Fortunately, the central government stepped in and took control and set the protocols for the rest of the world to follow. The doctor first sacrificed his freedom and then his life, soon dying from the disease that he had warned about. Happily, his intervention saved billions, a sacrifice that cannot be quantified even as the forked-tongue politicians claim ownership of the solutions that they often impeded. Yet, distracting global moral panics were engineered by foolish official statements and authorised idiocy. Amongst these were the early stage Chinese cover-up and whistleblower arrests, the much-denied offensive treatment of Africans in South China, the tit-for-tat endorsement of conspiracy theories alternatively holding the United States and China responsible for introducing the virus, and the doubling down on vituperative nationalisms to distract the populace in each country.

The real issue was insanitary culinary cultures and disrespect of ecological laws that can bring humankind to the brink of extinction, or at least, an anxious perception of it. For many, COVID-19 was the environment fighting back: chirping birds returned to Chinese cities where the sun could be again seen due to receding air pollution. Greenhouse gases declined significantly, the Himalayas could again be seen from northern India, governments offered tax holidays and allocated basic income grants, some landlords suspended their tenants' rent, and banks deferred housing bonds. Science and scientists regained popular ground over quackery, though the Centre for Disease Control really battled with White House myopia, a self-serving personal presidential culture that placed an entire country at risk for the sake of constituency rabble-rousing. For those who could work from home, broadband links further stressed the digital divide between rich and poor.

As *GroundUp* expressed it:

> Most important of all, we just might rediscover a sense of solidarity with each other, a 'we are all in this together' approach, which could break down some of the barriers in our own society. In some countries, young people are shopping for elderly and more vulnerable neighbours, leaving the parcels at their door. Instead of going out for the traditional evening walk, Italians are coming to their windows to sing together. Spending more time at home with families, and less time in malls and more on quiet walks, may help us rethink our consumerist ways for when this is all over. (email notice, 20 March 2020)

'But in inequitable South Africa,' *GroundUp* continued, 'rather than grabbing all the toilet paper and hand sanitisers from the supermarket shelves, we should be finding ways to share the wealth we have. Out of all this, a better society could emerge.'

That is why COVID-19 became the Gotcha agent of 2020. It revealed the price of extreme excess, punishing humans with a pandemic, global recession and social paranoia. The obverse is that crisis can bring about altruism and compassion, and a greater sense of social purpose. It offered a new way of reading Frantz Fanon's warnings about the need for social consciousness to guide and temper nationalism and put a break on predatory elites, the perpetrators of e-cow-nomics and their rapacious civil servants who often sabotage the national economy for their own pecuniary ends as they did all over Africa during the postcolonial phase, and especially during the astoundingly destructive Zuptanomics decade. For President Cyril Ramaphosa, the pandemic gave him the platform to finally step up to the wicket, to banish Zuptanomics, to restore law and order, and to create the conditions for a new society, his promised New Dawn, the one that was stillborn by the end of the 1990s.

Plagues drive change and bring about a new social vision, but they also popularly trade on pandemics of hate, hoarding and conspiracy.[2] But at social levels the crisis brought about major state investments in public goods, with states engaging in price control and appropriate distribution of basic commodities (like toilet paper, sanitisers and canned food). The crisis cautioned self-seeking behaviour, exposed serious gaps in non-Chinese heathcare systems and policies, and emphasised the interdependent nature of modern societies, economies and supply chains, communities, family units and of individuals. Telemedicine will move from the margins to centre stage in the advanced world, but the downside is that electronic pollution will skyrocket just as much as physical pollution receded. Netflix and YouTube downgraded the quality of their signals to lift pressure on the Internet.

Efficiently funded government at all levels is required, with restored public trust, and social support can be found in an instant even by bankrupt states. Despite Trump's denialism of science, and then his attempts to commoditise and rhetorically declare a vaccine, science became more open and popularly trusted. This response to the virus has the potential to change the world.[3]

Steph Sterling, vice-president of Advocacy and Policy at the Roosevelt Institute, observed the following:

> The coronavirus has laid bare the failures of our costly, inefficient, market-based system for developing, researching and manufacturing medicines and vaccines. COVID-19 is one of several coronavirus outbreaks we have

seen over the past 20 years, yet the logic of our current system – a range of costly government incentives intended to stimulate private-sector development – has resulted in the 18-month window we now anticipate before widespread vaccine availability. Private pharmaceutical firms simply will not prioritize a vaccine or other countermeasure for a future public health emergency until its profitability is assured, and that is far too late to prevent mass disruption.[4]

Has COVID-19 gotcha-ed us?

The environment when fighting back against human-led destruction will make critical cuts. Critical cuts will be incised when academics have had enough of the distractions imposed by autocracies that surveil and suppress rather than innovate, though these tend to occur in the arena of weak public spheres. We can write a lot, but changing things for the better is an uphill task as taking on blunderland run by the PoW, as well studied as it is, is always a daunting, and sometimes hazardous, affair. Cultural studies was once a critical cut; now it is just a syllabus; it was once a gotcha intervention, now it is an opaque epistemological code, as many of its post-structuralist adherents mystify through over-use of opaque language. All academic disciplines, however, can reclaim their rightful critical imperatives.

I have tried to conclude this book on something of a positive note and I have very much enjoyed writing it as a form of exorcism in dealing with academentia, and especially of my own life-long encounters with different kinds of blunderland. But, in keeping with the virus metaphor, again drawing on Martin (1973: 126–127), let me conclude thus: 'The bureaucratic virus, like its influenza counterpart, is extremely difficult to treat with any sort of vaccine, largely because vaccines are effective only against specific and individual mutations.'

While there is no magic bullet available in the struggle against blundering bureaucracy, understanding is the best means of navigating the terrain, and doing the best we can under the conditions in which we find ourselves. While academentia exists, the condition can be navigated, reigned in and critically examined. And making sense of it, appropriating it constructively and sometimes taming it can even be fun.

Notes

1. As Saunderson-Meyer observed, a positive aspect to disaster is that it usually up-ends conventional thinking. The imperative for urgency and improvisation removes the sapping burden of 'But Marx says…', 'But Keynes showed…' and 'We've always done it this way…' That kind of breaking of mental shackles has not happened here, so far. The Small Business Development minister allotted support to failing small and medium enterprises according to a geographic and demographic formula. In other words, not according to how badly support was needed or how effective it would be, but according to provincial and racial quotas (*Politicsweb*, 11 April 2020).

2. Read more at: https://www.abc.net.au/news/2020-03-20/coronavirus-conspiracy-theories-spreading-like-wildfire/12062516

3. Read more at: https://www.universityworldnews.com/post.php?story=20200318080659671

4. Read more at: https://www.politico.com/news/magazine/2020/03/19/coronavirus-effect-economy-life-society-analysis-covid-135579

References

Anderson B (1983) *Imagined communities: Reflections on the origin and spread of nationalism.* London: Verso

Anthony L (2009) *The elephant whisperer.* London: Pan Macmillan

Ardrey R (1966) *The territorial imperative.* New York: Atheneum

ASSAf (Academy of Science of South Africa) (2011) 'Consensus study on the state of the humanities in South Africa'. In *Status, prospects and strategies.* Pretoria: Academy of Science of South Africa

Baker SJ (2014) 'Stabilitas or mobilitas?' *The Institute for Sacred Architecture* 26: 31–33. http://www.sacredarchitecture.org/articles/stabilitas_or_mobilitas

Barnabas S (2011) 'Reflection on completion of a dissertation'. *SUBtext*: 8–9. http://ccms.ukzn.ac.za/files/articles/Subtext/subtext%20heritage%20 issue%202011.pdf

Basson A (2019) *Blessed by BOSASA: Inside Gavin Watson's state capture cult.* Cape Town: Jonathan Ball

Bethlehem L and Harris A (2012) 'Unruly pedagogies; migratory interventions: unsettling cultural studies'. *Critical Arts* 26(1): 3–13

Bodunrin I (2013) 'Reflecting on the warmth of cold Kalahari nights' *SUBtext*: 4–5. http://ccms.ukzn.ac.za/Libraries/staff-documents/subtext_ spring_2013.sflb.ashx

Bohannon J (2013) 'Who's afraid of peer review?' *Science* 342(6154): 60–65. https://science.sciencemag.org/content/342/6154/60.full

Booysen S (ed.) (2016) *Fees must fall: Decolonisation and governance in South Africa.* Johannesburg: Witwatersrand University Press

Boykoff M (2019) 'Leave 'em laughing instead of crying: Climate humor can break down barriers and find common ground'. *The Conversation*, 30 September. https://theconversation.com/leave-em-laughing-instead- of-crying-climate-humor-can-break-down-barriers-and-find-common- ground-120704

Brink C (2018) *The soul of a university: Why excellence is not enough.* Bristol: Bristol University Press

Bryson B (2000) *Down under*. New York: Doubleday

Buccus I (2019) 'Ace and the gang were precisely the people Fanon warned us about'. *Sunday Times*, 4 August

Chambers I (2014) 'Cultural studies under Mediterranean skies'. *Critical Arts* 28(5): 871–874

Chetty N and Merrett C (2014) *The struggle for the soul of a South African university: The University of KwaZulu-Natal: Academic freedom, corporatisation and transformation*. http://www.natalia.org.za/Files/Other%20books/SSSAU%20UKZN-BOOK.pdf

Cloete N (2015) 'The PhD and the ideology of "no transformation"'. *University World News*, 28 August. https://www.universityworldnews.com/post.php?story=20150827135017823

Connell K and Hilton M (eds) (2016) *Cultural studies 50 years on: History, practice and politics*. New York: Rowman and Littlefield

Darwin C (1859) *On the origin of species by means of natural selection, or the preservation of favoured races in the struggle for life*. London: John Murray

Dasnois A and Whitfield C (2019) *Paper tiger: Iqbal Survé and the downfall of Independent Newspapers*. Cape Town: Tafelberg

Dawkins R (2006) *The god delusion*. Boston: Mariner Books

De Lange RW (2015) 'Encounters with panaceas: Reading flyers and posters on "traditional" healing – a reply to Kadenge and Ndlovu (2012)'. *Journal of Contemporary African Studies* 33(4): 530–539

De Lange, RW (2017) 'Allopathic and traditional health practitioners: A reply to Nemutandani, Hendricks and Mulaudzi'. *African Journal of Primary Health Care & Family Medicine* 9(1): 1284

Derrida J (2008) *The animal that therefore I am*. Edited by Marie- Louise Mallet. New York: Fordham University Press

Dicks A (2014) 'On the subject of history: Making connections with the past'. *SUBtext*: 10. http://ccms.ukzn.ac.za/Libraries/articles/SUBtext_Winter_2014_Completed.sflb.ashx

Dyll L (2003) 'In the sun with Silikat'. *Current Writing* 15: 135–150

Dyll L (2012) 'Pondering the completion of a PhD thesis'. *SUBtext*: 3. http://
ccms.ukzn.ac.za/files/articles/Subtext/subtext%20kalahari%202012%20
web.pdf

Eagleton T (2006) 'Lunging, flailing, mispunching'. *London Review of Books*
28(20). http://www.lrb.co.uk/v28/n20/terry-eagleton/lunging-flailing-
mispunching

Evans S (2020) 'Coronavirus has finally made us recognise the illegal wildlife
trade is a public health issue'. *The Conversation*, 18 March. https://
theconversation.com/coronavirus-has-finally-made-us-recognise-the-illegal-
wildlife-trade-is-a-public-health-issue-133673

Fanon F (1963) *The wretched of the earth*. Harmondsworth: Penguin

Feyerabend, P (1975/2010) *Against method*. 4th ed. New York: Verso Books

Frassinelli PP (2020) 'Crisis? Which crisis? The humanities reloaded'. *Critical
Arts* 33(3): 1–15

Freire P (2005) *Pedagogy of the oppressed*. New York: Continuum

Gaonkar DP (2002) 'Toward new imaginaries: An introduction'. *Public Culture*
14(1): 1–19

Goldin I and Muggah R (2020) 'The world before this coronavirus and after
cannot be the same'. *The Conversation*, 21 March. https://theconversation.
com/the-world-before-this-coronavirus-and-after-cannot-be-the-
same-134905

Gqubule T (2017) *No longer whispering to power: The story of Thuli Madonsela*. Cape
Town: Jonathan Ball

Grant J (2012) 'A hollow sound of lamentation'. *SUBText*: 1–2. http://ccms.ukzn.
ac.za/files/articles/Subtext/subtext%20winter%202012%20web.pdf

Gray B (2016) 'Neoliberalising higher education: Language and performing
purpose in corporatized'. *Critical Arts* 30(5): 745–750

Greer G (1999) *A new introduction to journalism*. Cape Town: Juta

Habermas J (1971) *Knowledge and human interests: A general perspective*. Boston:
Beacon Press

Habib A (2019) *Rebels and rage: Reflecting on #Feesmustfall*. Cape Town: Jonathan Ball

Harford T (2006) *The undercover economist*. Oxford: Oxford University Press

Hartshorne R (1959) *Perspective on the nature of geography*. Dunfermline: Better World Books

Hartstone-Rose A and Stynder DD (2013) 'Hypercarnivory, durophagy or generalised carnivory in the Mio-Pliocene hyaenids of South Africa?' *South African Journal of Science* 109(5/6): 1–10

Heleta S (2016) 'Academics can change the world – if they stop talking only to their peers'. *The Conversation*, 9 March. https://theconversation.com/academics-can-change-the-world-if-they-stop-talking-only-to-their-peers-55713

Holman Jones S, Adams TE, Ellis C (eds) (2013) *The Handbook of Autoethnography*. California: Left Coast Books

Jansen J (2020) 'Racket science: How cheating SA academics snaffle research millions'. *Times Select*, 20 February. https://select.timeslive.co.za/ideas/2020-02-20-racket-science-how-cheating-sa-academics-snaffle-research-millions/

Johnston A (2014) *South Africa: Inventing the nation*. London: Bloomsbury

Joubert JJ (2019) *Will South Africa be okay? 17 key questions*. Cape Town: Tafelberg

Joyner J (2010). 'Putting a price on professors'. *Outside the Beltway*, 24 October. https://www.outsidethebeltway.com/putting-a-price-on-professors/

Kant I (1998) *Critique of pure reason*. Cambridge: Cambridge University Press

Keegan T (1996) *Colonial South Africa and the origins of the racial order*. London: Leicester University Press

Keynes JM (1936) *The general theory of employment, interest and money*. London: Palgrave Macmillan

Krige F (2019) *The SABC 8*. Cape Town: Penguin Random House

Laurence JP and Hull R (1969) *The Peter principle: Why things go wrong*. New York: William Morrow & Company

Levitt SD and Dubner SJ (2006) *Freakonomics: A rogue economist explores the hidden side of everything*. Harmondsworth: Penguin

Levitt SD and Dubner SJ (2009) *Super freakonomics: Global cooling, patriotic prostitutes and why suicide bombers should buy life insurance*. New York: Harper Collins

Lodge D (2011) *The campus trilogy*. London: Vintage Books

Logie B (2011) 'Kalahari capers'. *SUBtext*: 3. http://ccms.ukzn.ac.za/files/
articles/Subtext/subtext%20heritage%20issue%202011.pdf

Makgoba MW and Chetty D (2010) 'The history and context of higher education
in South Africa post-1994'. In MW Makgoba and JC Mubangizi (eds)
*The creation of the University of KwaZulu-Natal: Reflections on a merger and
transformation experience.* New Delhi: Excel Books

Martin TL (1973) *Malice in blunderland.* New York: McGraw Hill Higher
Education

Martin TL (2004) *Poiesis and possible worlds: A study in modality and literary theory.*
Toronto: University of Toronto Press

Mbatha Z (2013) 'A publishing interlude: Authenticity and contemporaneity'.
SUBtext: 10. http://ccms.ukzn.ac.za/files/articles/Subtext/subtextautumn2013.pdf

Mbeki M (2009) *Architects of poverty: Why African capitalism needs changing.*
Johannesburg: Picador Africa

Mboti N (2012) 'Writing in the San/d'. *SUBtext*: 16. http://ccms.ukzn.ac.za/
files/articles/Subtext/subtext%20kalahari%202012%20web.pdf

Miya M (2013) 'Impression from the McGregor Museum'. *SUBtext*: 1–2. http://
ccms.ukzn.ac.za/files/articles/subtext_winter_2013.pdf

Mosco V (1996) *The political economy of communication.* New York: Sage

Mouton J and Valentine A (2017) 'The extent of SA-authored articles in predatory
journals'. *South African Journal of Science* 113(7/8). http://www.sajs.co.za/
system/tdf/publications/pdf/SAJS-113-7-8_Mouton_ResearchArticle.
pdf?file=1&type=node&id=35779&force

Mthombothi B (2019) 'Black lives seem not to matter when those dying are
young men sacrificed in the name of culture'. *Sunday Times*, 29 December.
https://www.timeslive.co.za/sunday-times/opinion-and-analysis/2019-
12-29-black-lives-seem-not-to-matter-when-those-dying-are-young-men-
sacrificed-in-the-name-of-culture-/

Myburgh P-L (2017) *The Republic of Gupta: A story of state capture.* Cape Town:
Penguin Random House

Myburgh P-L (2019) *Gangster state: Unravelling Ace Magashule's web of capture.*
Cape Town: Penguin Random House

Ndebele NS (2017) 'They are burning memory'. *Critical Arts* 31(1): 102–109

Ngcobo N (2014) 'Unlocking the historical codes of the KwaZulu-Natal battlefields'. *SUBtext*: 1–3. http://ccms.ukzn.ac.za/Libraries/articles/ SUBtext_Winter_2014_Completed.sflb.ashx

Njisane A (2012) 'My Kalahari experience. Shifting experiences'. *SUBtext*: 4–7. http://ccms.ukzn.ac.za/files/articles/Subtext/subtext%20kalahari%20 2012%20web.pdf

Olver C (2017) *How to steal a city: The battle for Nelson Mandela Bay: An inside account*. Cape Town: Jonathan Ball

Oliver P (1970) *Savannah syncopators: African retentions in the blues*. London: Studio Vista

Pauw J (2017) *The president's keepers: Those keeping Zuma in power and out of prison*. Cape Town: Tafelberg

Pinker S (2014) 'Why academics stink at writing'. *The Chronicle of Higher Education*, 26 September. http://stevenpinker.com/files/pinker/files/why_ academics_stink_at_writing.pdf

Player I (1998) *Zulu wilderness: Shadow and soul*. Cape Town: New Africa Books

Ramgobin M (n.d.) *The people shall govern: An overview of the Freedom Charter*. CCMS Occasional Paper Number 2

Readings B (1997) *The university in ruins*. Cambridge: Harvard University Press

Reich CA (1970) 'Reflections: The greening of America'. *The New Yorker*, 26 September

Robinson G (2010) 'Academics: Researchers or teachers?' *SUBtext*: 6–7. http:// ccms.ukzn.ac.za/files/articles/Subtext/subtext%20winter2010.pdf

Rolfe G (2014) 'We are all para-academics now'. In A Wardrop, DM Withers and G Rolfe (eds) *The para-academic handbook: A toolkit for making-learning-creating-acting*. Bristol: HammerOn Press

Ryle G (1963) *The concept of mind*. Harmondsworth: Peregrine

Sadomba ZW (2011) *War veterans in Zimbabwe's revolution: Challenging neo-colonialism and settler and international capital*. Martlesham: James Currey

Saunderson-Meyer W (2017) 'Political correctness is more stifling than religious dogma'. *Politicsweb*, 24 March. http://www.politicsweb.co.za/opinion/making-treason-out-of-reason

Saunderson-Meyer W (2020) 'Covid's South African score is not cheery tune'. *Politicsweb*, 11 April. https://www.politicsweb.co.za/opinion/covid19s-south-african-score-is-not-a-cheery-tune

Serper A (2014) 'Democratic education practices in South Africa: A critical reflection on a dialogic perspective'. In V Byczkiewicz (ed.) *Democracy & education: Collected perspectives*. Los Angeles. Trébol Press

Shah S (2020) 'Pandemic: Tracking contagions from cholera to Ebola and beyond'. *Politico*, 19 March. https://www.politico.com/news/magazine/2020/03/19/coronavirus-effect-economy-life-society-analysis-covid-135579#econ

Shepperson A (1993) 'Can SA culture be cured?' *SUBtext*: 1, 4. http://ccms.ukzn.ac.za/files/articles/Publications/sub%20text%20no.%205,%201996.pdf

Shepperson A (2008) 'Safety-culture and the logic of hazard'. *Critical Arts* 22(2): 187–234

Sloan AP (1967) *My years with General Motors*. New York: MacFadden-Bartell

Smith A (ed.) (1986) *Ethnicity and nationalism*. Leiden: EJ Brill

Sterne J (2002) 'Cultural policy studies and the problem of political representation'. *The Communication Review* 5: 59–89

Styan J-B (2015) *Blackout: The Eskom crisis*. Pretoria: Lapa Publishers

Styan J-B (2018) *Steinhoff: Inside SA's biggest corporate crash*. Pretoria: Lapa Publishers

Styan J-B and Vecchiatto P (2019) *The Bosasa billions: How the ANC sold its soul for braaipacks, booze and bags of cash*. Pretoria: Lapa Publishers

Sundaram R (2018) *Indentured: Behind the scenes at Gupta TV*. Johanneburg: Jacana Media

Swilling M (comp.) (2017) *Betrayal of the promise: How South Africa is being stolen*. http://pari.org.za/wp-content/uploads/2017/05/Betrayal-of-the-Promise-25052017.pdf

Teer-Tomaselli RE (2011) 'Transforming state-owned enterprises in the global age: Lessons from broadcasting and telecommunications in South Africa'. In A Olorunnisola and KG Tomaselli (eds) *Political economy of media transformation in South Africa*. Cresskill: Hampton Press

Tomaselli KG (2018) 'Where does my body belong?' In L Turner, NP Short, A Grant and TE Adams (eds) *International perspectives on autoethnographic research and practice*. London: Routledge

Tomaselli KG (2019) *Making sense of research*. Pretoria: Van Schaik

Tomaselli KG and Caldwell M (2019) 'Corporate communication: Adversarial, transmission, dialogical'. *Communicatio* 45(2): 56–80

Tomaselli KG and Mpofu A (1997) 'The re-articulation of meaning in national monuments: Beyond apartheid'. *Culture and Policy* 8(3): 57–86

Tomaselli KG and Ramgobin M (1988) 'Culture and conservation: Whose interests?' In I Coetzee and G-M van der Waal (eds) *The conservation of culture: Context and challenges: Proceedings of the South African conference on the conservation of culture, Cape Town, 6–10 June 1988*. Pretoria: Conference organisers

Tomaselli KG and Sakarombe P (2015) 'Griots, satirical columns, and the micro-public sphere'. *Journal of African Media Studies* 7(3): 315–328

Tomaselli KG and Shepperson A (2011) 'Mirror communities and straw individualisms: Essentialism, cinema and semiotic analysis'. *Journal of African Cinemas* 3(1): 3–24

Townsend R (1970) *Up the organization: How to stop the organization from stifling people and strangling profits*. New York: Knopf

Tucker L (2016) *Mystery of the white lions: Children of the sun god*. California: Hay House

Vogler C (2002) 'Social imaginary, ethics and methodological individualism'. *Public Culture* 14(3): 625–627

Wardrop A, Withers DM and Rolfe G (eds) (2014) *The para-academic handbook. A toolkit for making-learning-creating-acting*. Bristol: HammerOn Press

Watson C (2016) 'An education in irony: Why academics need to be funny'. *The Conversation*, 4 April. https://theconversation.com/an-education-in-irony-why-academics-need-to-be-funny-55261

Wels H (2013) 'Whispering empathy: Transdisciplinary reflections on research methodology'. In B Musschenga and A van Harskamp (eds) *What makes us moral? On the capacities and conditions for being moral*. Dordrecht: Springer

Wittemyer G (2020) 'The new coronavirus emerged from the global wildlife trade – and may be devastating enough to end it'. *Colorado State University Magazine*, 1 April. https://source.colostate.edu/the-new-coronavirus-emerged-from-the-global-wildlife-trade-and-may-be-devastating-enough-to-end-it/

Zille H (2017) 'White-bashing cancer destroys SA from within, says Zille'. *Sunday Times*, 30 April. https://www.timeslive.co.za/sunday-times/opinion-and-analysis/2017-04-30-white-bashing-cancer-destroys-sa-from-within-says-zille/

Index